KHUMBU
Nepal

ALUN RICHARDSON

FOREWORD

The wonderful Khumbu Himal has played a big part in my life. The first time I visited was in 1962 to climb the South Face of Nuptse. I subsequently made two trips, in 1972 and 1975 to the South West Face of Everest and finally in 1985 I climbed Everest via the South Col.

My generation were lucky, the major peaks had hardly been touched and the number of expeditions were small, we had the mountain largely to ourselves, we laid the fixed ropes down and Sherpas supported the climbing teams. Expeditions to the Himalayas in the 1960 and 1970s required 8 to 9 weeks or more just to get to the mountain. The biggest challenge was the huge logistical effort, with large teams of porters, Sherpas and yaks needed to get the equipment and mountaineers into place for the climbs.

Not long after our forays onto the bigger faces on the biggest of mountains, expeditions gradually became smaller, but it wasn't until the mid to late 70s that 8000m peaks were climbed in light and fast 'Alpine' style. Messner, in 1978, along with Peter Habeler changed climbing when they summited Everest without supplemental oxygen. Messner went on to do it solo. He was the first real modern climber and he opened the doors for the incredibly bold, alpine style ascents now being done all over the Himalaya.

Everest has been a magnet for me, it has drawn me back again and again and finally getting to the top aged 50 meant a lot to me. It was a wonderful experience and got Everest out of my system. I got to the top using every trick in the book, much like mountaineers on today's commercial expeditions. I had a superb Sherpa team, we used oxygen from 7000m and one strapping Sherpa carried my spare bottle to 8400m, so I was helped in every possible way. Everest ascents get slagged horribly these days, but it is actually a fantastic and beautiful route, if only it didn't have so many people.

When I first visited Khumbu there were few visitors, but increasing tourism and mountaineering has had an impact on the people who live there, but on the whole I believe it to be beneficial. It's about balance – areas of Khumbu are being modernised with electricity, nightclubs, internet cafes and everything else, that's just the way of things and there's not much point in regretting it. The communities of the Khumbu have improved their standard of living considerably and it is an almost inevitable development. I think that one of the traps we fall into is saying that there are these wonderful quaint Sherpa people living in their little villages and I don't want it to change. But I think that the development that's happening, needs to happen and is going to happen anyway, what is important is how the Sherpa people handle it. I think they are very sophisticated and resilient, remember they are a very old civilisation, slightly older than our own. Some younger Sherpas may be confused, as in fact an awful lot of young westerners are, but it's all part of progress. To reduce the numbers of people visiting Khumbu would not be welcomed because the Sherpas have built an economy around tourism and significantly they have built the economy themselves.

Khumbu is a wonderful place – I not only loved the mountains and the scenery, but I also made life long Sherpa friends. I can only hope that the inevitable changes coming from global warming and tourism will be sympathetic to the people, the culture and the environment.

Sir Chris Bonington

INTRODUCTION

Thirty years ago I visited the Khumbu Himal for the first time and fell in love with its breathtaking mountain scenery, the people and their culture. I have returned many times as a Mountain Guide and photographer, climbed some of its peaks, followed many of its trails and passes and made some very good friends.

In 2015 I worked for the Mountain Trust Charity, photographing the journey of three handmade watches being taken to the summit of Chomolungmu (Everest) by the Royal Gurkha regiment. During that same year, two devastating earthquakes rocked Nepal, killing 9000 people and destroying property high and low. The earthquakes not only decimated Nepal it also stopped the 2015 Gurkha expedition when an avalanche ripped through Everest Base Camp (EBC) killing 17 people and injuring many more! But Gurkhas are resilient and I was honoured to be selected as the 'Official Photographer' to the Royal Gurkha Regiment's 2017 Mount Everest Expedition that put thirteen serving Gurkhas on the summit. The two expeditions and months training with them gave me an insight into the wonderful Gurkha soldiers and on my return I started to raise money for the Gurkha Welfare Trust (GWT) through selling images and giving talks to camera clubs. Nepal is one of the poorest countries in the world and therefore seventy percent of the profit from this book goes to the GWT, which gives 100% to the people of Nepal.

I never tire of Khumbu's spectacular mountains, its raging torrents, the flowers in spring, the occasional sightings of tahr or musk deer and of course the people. Few mountain regions have brought me to tears, but standing on a high pass or summit looking over Khumbu is one of them. It is understandably a top destination for trekkers following the EBC trail, but there is much more to Khumbu for those willing to look into different valleys and passes.

Khumbu is a fragile place and there are challenges ahead, but whatever the future brings for the Sherpa people, their culture and the environment, it will always remain very special. It is somewhere everyone should experience at least once – to walk quietly amongst the highest mountains on earth is humbling.

This book is a photographic celebration of the stunning surroundings and provides a voice for the people I have come to admire, I hope it inspires you to visit or reminds you of where you have been.

Alun Richardson

"A hundred divine epochs would not suffice to describe all the marvels of the Himalaya."

SANSKRIT PROVERB

Chomolungmu

Nepalis call it Sagarmatha "Goddess of the sky"
Tibetans call it Chomolungmu, Quomolungma or
Jomolungma – "goddess mother of the world"
English speakers call it Everest.

THE KHUMBU HIMAL

The Khumbu Himal is the upper part of the Solu Khumbu region, a district in northeastern Nepal. It is named after a sacred peak high above the villages of Khumjung and Khunde – Khumbila (5761m).

On the western side of Khumbu, the 'Himalayan' mountain chain stretches westwards and blends into the Kararkorum and the Hindu Kush ranges. To the east sits the other wordly Sikkim, Bhutan and Eastern India and on the northern border some of the highest mountains on earth – Chomolungmu, Lhotse Shar and Cho Oyu form a barrier that separates Nepal from Tibet.

Glaciers emerge from these high peaks and feed two rivers – the Bhote Kosi and the Dudh Kosi – that have carved deep valleys and jagged ridges. The two rivers combine at Khumbu's southern tip and continue their journey through Nepal's middle hills and the terai or lowlands to reach India.

It is a harsh place to live, but also a very beautiful landscape that is looked after by the Sherpa people – the custodians of the region – whose culture and warm hospitality make it such a welcoming place.

The majority of visitors come to gaze upon the mountains, but there is more to Khumbu than that. Khumbu is a sacred place for the Sherpas and understanding how their relationship has helped shape the mountains makes it a much more interesting place to travel through.

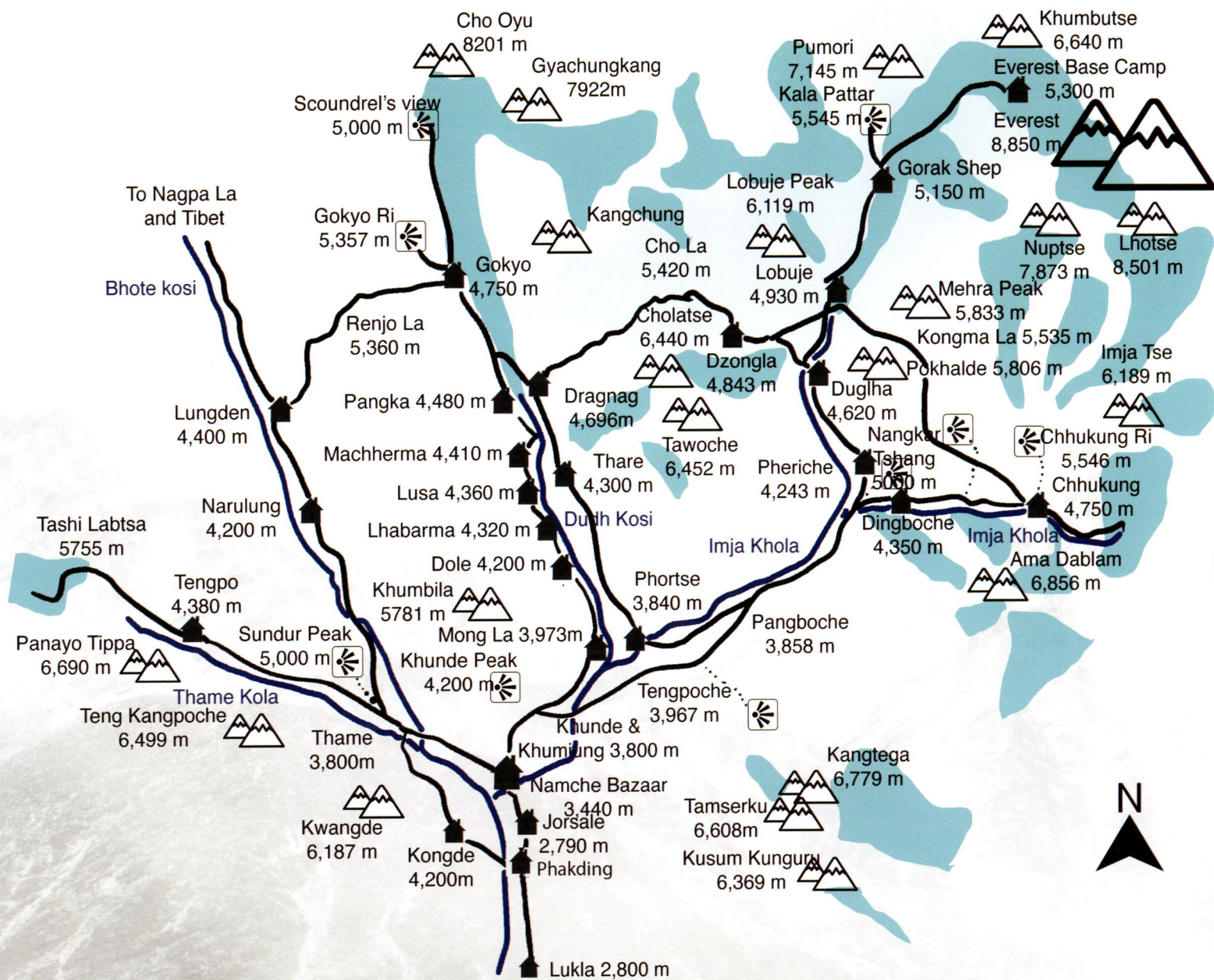

Jomo Miyo Langsangma

Khumbu is home to the Buddhist goddess Jomo Miyo Langsangma who resides in an ice palace on top of Chomolungmu. One of five beautiful sisters, she was something of a demoness in her younger days. Over time she mellowed and today she is celebrated for her generosity and grants the wishes of those who are most deserving and in Khumbu, nobody is more deserving than the Sherpa people.

"They paved paradise and put up a parking lot

With a pink hotel, a boutique, and a swinging hot spot

Don't it always seem to go

That you don't know what you got 'til it's gone?

They paved paradise and put up a parking lot

They took all the trees and put 'em in a tree museum

And they charged the people a dollar and a half to see them

No, no, no

Don't it always seem to go

That you don't know what you got 'til it's gone?

They paved paradise and put up a parking lot"

JONI MITCHELL

SAGARMATHA NATIONAL PARK

From 1846 Nepal was a "forbidden land", allowing only small businesses, Indian pilgrims and close British friends to enter. Towards the end of Rana's rule in 1951 and the start of democracy, Nepal opened its doors to visitors. The first trekker was Bill Tilman in 1949 who got permission to make several treks and then Maurice Herzog led an early expedition to Annapurna in 1950. Since then mountain tourism has exploded, changing the country's profile, no more than in Khumbu. It is estimated that 20 tourists visited in 1964, but in 2019 it was 60,000 not including support staff, guides and porters. Add to this the influx of non Sherpas from the middle hill and lowland areas in search of work, plus the non Sherpa government workers – teachers, National Park employees and army personnel and there is a lot of people pressure!

The Sagarmatha National Park covering 1148 sq km was established in 1976 with the challenge of supporting the fragile Khumbu environment, yet attracting more tourists and increasing revenue – a difficult balancing act. The good thing is that the financial contribution visitors make is helping the park to protect the environment. The natural heritage of the mountains, glaciers, deep valleys and seven peaks over 7000 m was recognised by UNESCO as a World Heritage Site in 1979.

The Sagarmatha Pollution Control Committee (SPCC) was established by the local Sherpa people in 1991 to manage the growing waste problem. Since 1997, their role has grown and SPCC now also set the climbing route through the Khumbu Icefall (gateway to climbing Everest) and check climbing permits, monitor illegal climbing and implement waste management strategies at the base camps of the Khumbu area's mountains and peaks.

SHERPA LANGUAGE

The Sherpa language is an ancient Tibetan dialect that has developed in its own way for 500 years. It is only a spoken language and although there have been attempts to introduce a written form it is not an easy undertaking. The spellings in this book are directly from my Sherpa friends and reflect how they speak.

WEL COME TO

Sagarmatha National Park
World Heritage Natural Site
(Estd. in 1976)

MALE HIMALAYAN TAHR

The traditional culture and religious practices of Tibetan Buddhists include the restriction of animal hunting and slaughtering as well as reverence of all living beings. Consequently there is a lot of wildlife in the Khumbu, such as the rarely seen snow leopard, bears, musk deer and bearded vultures.

FEMALE HIMALAYAN TAHR WITH YOUNG

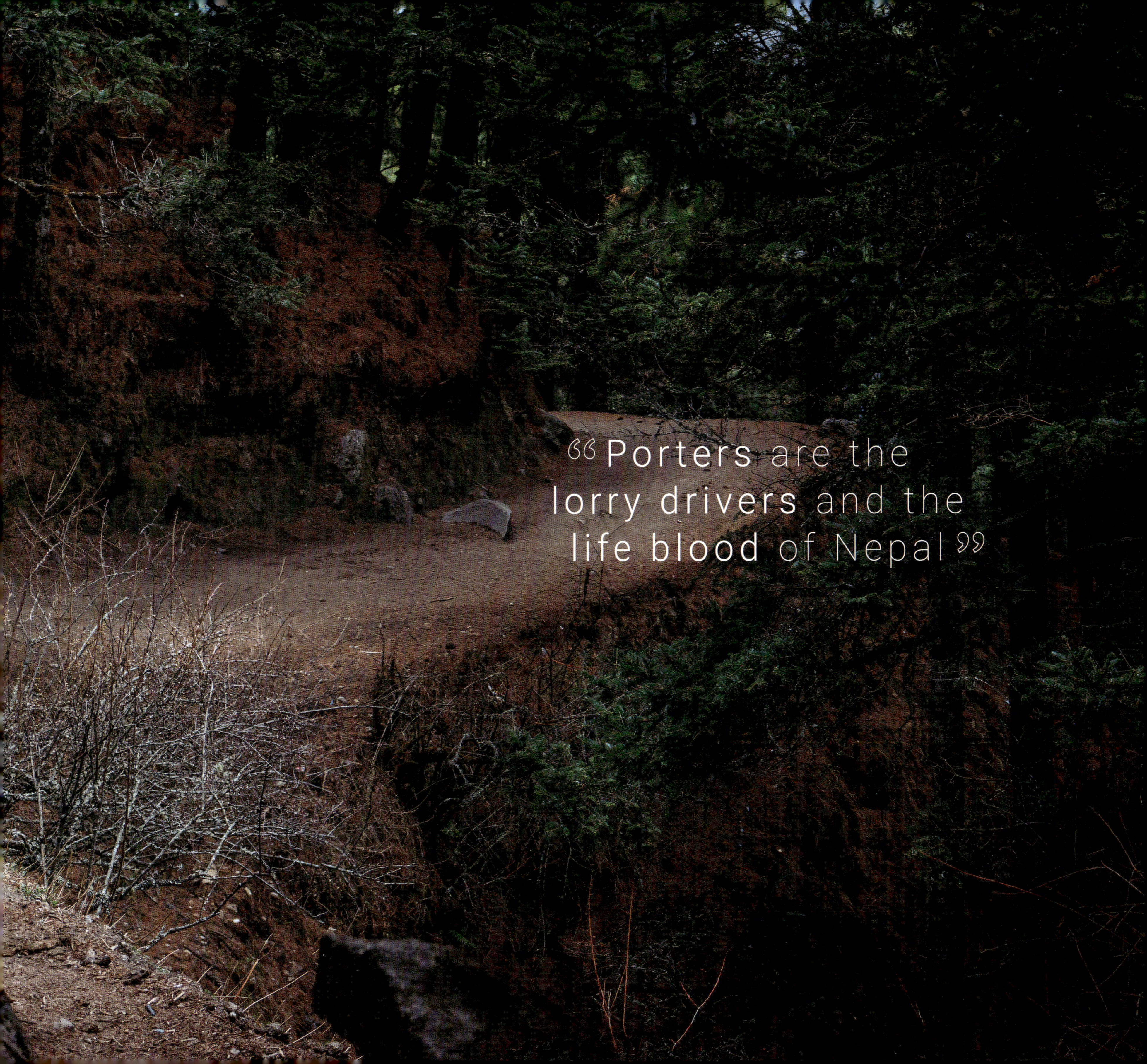

“Porters are the lorry drivers and the life blood of Nepal”

'SHANGRI LA'

Sherpas believe in the existence of hidden mountain valleys called "beyuls" – earthly paradises created by Guru Rinpoche, founder of the Nyingma school of Buddhism. In these sacred realms, enlightened followers can find peace, free from suffering, poverty, disease, and injustice. At the heart of Sherpa beliefs is a deep reverence for nature, protected by mountain deities and spirits. This has fostered centuries of sustainable practices such as protecting forests, keeping waters clean, and respecting all living creatures. Perhaps Shangri-La truly lies nestled within the world's tallest peaks.

The Khumbu beyul's cultural influence should remain a cornerstone of environmental conservation, but it is in danger of being replaced by regulations and policing. Sagarmatha National Park is trying to embrace this legacy, involving Sherpa leaders in Buffer-Zone user groups to ensure that local voices are heard. I hope they listen. A positive development is the Sacred Sites Trail project which aims to protect important spiritual landmarks while promoting responsible tourism.

Phinjo Sherpa, (a social worker with INGOs focused on social development in Nepal), shares advice for visitors: "Respect local customs: ask permission before taking photos, remove your shoes when entering homes or monasteries, and use respectful language. Support the community by dining in local restaurants, staying in Sherpa-owned lodges, and hiring local guides.

Engage in cultural experiences, like attending festivals or learning traditional crafts, and follow 'leave no trace' principles to minimise environmental impact. Carry reusable water bottles, avoid single-use plastics, and dispose of waste properly. Be adaptable and patient – things may not always go as planned."

Other recommendations are to take batteries and medications home, minimise hot showers, and opt for composting toilets over flushing toilets, which can pollute rivers. Instead of random gifts, consider donating to local or international charities, which better supports the whole community.

Experiencing Khumbu is different from merely seeing it. Following trails like a commodity on a conveyor belt, with hot showers, internet, and imported goods, risks losing the essence of Khumbu. While western amenities bring economic benefits for some, they may undermine the traditions and environmental values that have sustained the Sherpas and Khumbu for centuries.

The challenge is to find balance between modernisation and preservation, ensuring that Khumbu's unique culture and pristine landscapes remain protected for generations. By following local guidance from Sherpas like Phinjo, trekkers can experience a deeper, more respectful, and environmentally conscious journey through one of the most awe-inspiring places on earth.

"Khumbu is a holy place, our religion says that in the future when the world is in a war or pandemic and the world and people are in trouble and chaos, the place to hide, to take refuge, is Khumbu. That is why Khumbu is as important to us as our own life and I deeply love Khumbu."

YESHI LODGE OWNER IN NAMCHE

'Passing Tshering Sherpa' – this painting depicts global warming.

GLOBAL WARMING

"Sherpas are aware of global warming – weather patterns are becoming unpredictable with warmer winters, less snowfall, erratic rainfall, droughts and floods. This affects the growing of traditional crops because they depend on consistent seasonal conditions. Villages relying on glacier-fed rivers for agriculture and daily needs are finding that reduced water harms crop production, livestock, and the supply of drinking water.

4.7% of Sagarmatha park is covered by glaciers and Increased glacial melt is leading to the expansion of glacial lakes, which have burst with devastating floods. Thawing permafrost is causing landslides, soil erosion, destabilising mountain slopes and snow and ice slopes are now much less reliable. Additionally, unique plant and animal species adapted to the cold are moving to higher altitudes to find suitable habitats, which disrupts local ecosystems and puts some species at risk of extinction.

In my opinion global warming is big problem not only to the people in Khumbu, but also plants and animals – we can save the planet for our children and our children's children – for this we need wisdom, courage and compassion".

PHINJO SHERPA

Khumbu is home to a fluctuating population of 3500 Sherpas, spread among 20 villages. The Sherpa people are a small ethnic group in Nepal known for their humility and warmth. Their Buddhist beliefs are rooted in reincarnation and they see everyone as part of a journey towards enlightenment. This is reflected in the Nepali phrase 'Atithi Devo Bhava' – meaning 'Guest equals God' this underscores their duty to offer whatever one has to a guest.

Lhakpa Sonam Sherpa (www.sherpa-culture.com.np) reflects on the history of the Sherpa people.

"The name "Sherpa" derives from the Tibetan word "Sharpa," meaning "people from the east." Sherpas originally migrated from Tibet's Kham region in the late 14th century, crossing the Tashi Labtsa from the Rolwaling Valley and later the Nangpa La, initially settling near Pangboche, the site of Khumbu's oldest monastery. As glaciers receded, they moved deeper into the Khumbu region.

However, they may not have been the first in Khumbu; Rai herders from Solu had burned forests to clear grazing land, and local healers gathered medicinal plants in the area.

In their early years, Sherpas relied on livestock, farming and trade, journeying over high passes to exchange goods with Tibet and India. They grew barley, small amounts of peas, Tibetan radishes, tulips, cabbage, and carrots, while rice, maize, and millet were bartered for Tibetan goods such as salt, sheep's wool, yak tails, and puppies. Yaks were herded by men, who also used them for trade with Tibet, though these routes are now closed by China to limit Tibetan migration.

Early Sherpa settlements were above 3400m, but in summer, they moved as high as 5000m, with their herds grazing even higher at around 5500m. Before 1950, Sherpas relied on the Indian border for materials to build homes, make tools, and dye wool. Clothes were handwoven from yak hair and sheep wool, and household and farm work was – and still is – primarily managed by women.

After 1950, the arrival of trekkers and mountaineers introduced a new era, but Sherpas had been involved in mountaineering and trekking much earlier, working for Indian expeditions from Darjeeling. The first Sherpa to join a mountaineering expedition was A.M. Kalash in the Sikkim Himalaya in 1907, and later in the Kanchenjunga region in 1909. Since then, Sherpas have supported expeditions across India, Tibet, and Nepal. Notably, Pasang Kikuli, one of the first prominent Sherpas, who died in 1939 while rescuing a stranded climber on K2.

Before 1980, Sherpas led traditional lives, but with increased tourism came rapid change. Homes became lodges, and herdsmen became mountaineers and trekking guides, often using their livestock to transport supplies. Traditional family roles shifted, Western clothing became common, and cheap clothing from India and China replaced traditional attire. Many families left behind grass and potato fields to migrate to urban areas or abroad, resulting in a decline in cattle and a shortage of manure for crops. Today, most men work in trekking and mountaineering, while women manage lodges. Sherpa children often excel in school, with some studying abroad, while others return to work in tourism, fostering hope that their culture will endure. Religious festivals also play a role in keeping beliefs alive, even amid modernisation. While Buddhism remains strong, the tradition of becoming monks or lamas may be declining, which is concerning since lamas perform essential rites for the sick and deceased, especially for Sherpas who pass away in the mountains.

These are just some of the changes impacting the people of Khumbu. Tourism has brought prosperity, but along with it, both gains and losses to Sherpa culture and lifestyle."

Lhakpa Sonam Sherpa began studying Sherpa history and mountaineering in 1982. In 1994, he initiated the construction of the Sherpa Culture Museum and Mount Everest Documentation Center in Namche Bazaar, which opened in 2023. He hopes these efforts will inspire future generations to honour and preserve their heritage while navigating the challenges of a modernised world.

THE PEOPLE OF KHUMBU

"Farming has traditionally been a subsistence agriculture, with crops suited to the harsh mountain environment. However, money from relatives working abroad or in tourism have reduced the dependency on farming, resulting in some land being left fallow as fewer families rely on agriculture for food or income.

Potatoes, introduced in the 19th century, have become a staple crop because they thrive in the cold and poor soil. Barley and buckwheat, once common, have disappeared in most areas. These changes are driven partly by global warming, but also economic changes. Greenhouses are now used to protect crops from frost and tourism has shifted crops towards cabbage, carrots, onions, and herbs, which are sold to tourist lodges. With improved transportation, much of the food consumed in the region is now imported from Solu or Kathmandu."

PHINJO SHERPA

Religious and cultural rituals, for births, marriages, and death have remained largely unchanged for Sherpas.

Sherpa society is divided into 'ru' (clans) and Sherpas choose their own marriage partners outside their ru. The process of marriage may take several years – following a betrothal or engagement (sodene), the boy has the right to live with his fiancée in her parents' house. This may continue for several years, during which time the relationship can be ended. Once the families feel that the marriage will be successful, a wedding date is fixed (trichang) and a ceremony is carried out to confirm the marriage agreement (demchang), zendi' is the final ceremony where the woman lives with the man.

FAMILY LIFE

"The elderly are highly respected members of the community and are generally well cared for. This time in life is seen as a period of prayer, meditation and relaxation."

Sherpa families are small with households consisting of parents and their unmarried children. A newly married son may receive a house on completion of the marriage. Interestingly, a man does not return home until he has a child; he lives with his in-laws until such time as his wife gives birth. Marriages are monogamous, although having more than one husband is permitted and in the past was considered prestigious, it is non-existent today. Divorce is rare.

When someone dies, Lamas perform rituals to generate positive energy for the deceased. The heat of the body is thought to leave through the feet, hands, eyes, nose, ears, mouth, and the top of the head. The spirit of the dead person follows the same direction. If the spirit of the dead leaves from elsewhere, it is believed that the next life will be bad. If it comes out through the nose or eyes they reincarnate as an animal or person. If it leaves from the head they may go to heaven – 'Dewachen'.

There are many customs to a funeral, but usually the body is kept for three days then cremated. The ashes are made into 'tsatsa' and after 49 days they are left in a chorten or under a large rock.

After cremation a lama performs a ritual (Dun-tsig) at the deceased's home once a week for seven weeks. Within three or four weeks, the family makes offerings called Sheto for between three and fifteen days, depending on the family finances. Every evening, the family puts a tsampa on the embers of the fire and offers food and drink to family and friends.

When high Lamas and Rinpoches (older, respected, learned Lamas) die, they have special rituals performed and the body is cremated in a special chamber.

FUNERALS

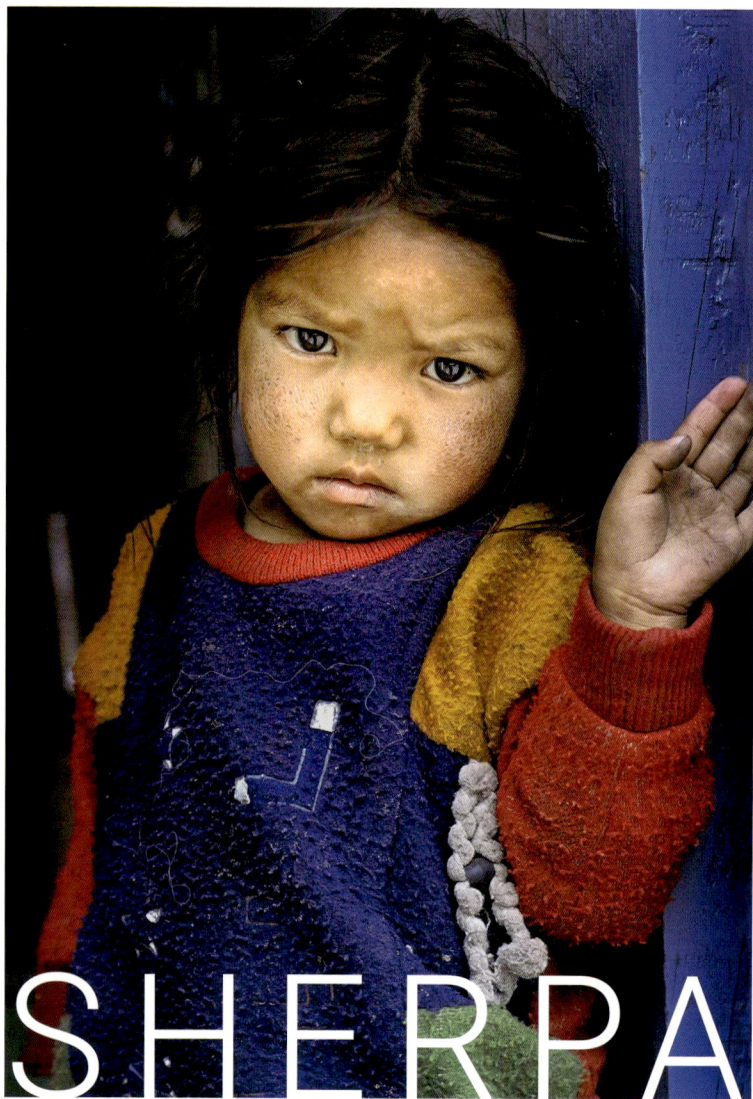

When a child is born the local Lama is informed of the date and time. Children are usually brought up by their mothers, as the men are often away for much of the year. Women are 'equal' in Sherpa society, however young girls are introduced to household chores at an early age, while boys have greater freedom for leisure and play! Even when adult, women are rarely seen outside, but this is changing as Sherpas experience new influences. Boys undergo an initiation ceremony between seven and nine years of age, which is presided over by a Lama and accompanied by feasting and drinking.

Children are frequently named after the day of the week on which they were born. Sunday is Nima and the following days are Dawa, Mingma, Lakpa, Phurba, Pasang and Pemba. They often add the prefix Ang to the name similar to the suffix son or junior. You would call Ang Nima, Nima but never Ang. The second name is chosen from a wide range of male or female names with meanings such as 'fortunate one' or 'long life', for boys or 'healthy' and 'joyful' or 'wise one', for girls. In Nepal it is common to keep the name of one's ethnic group e.g. Sherpa as a surname or in some case their occupations.

SHERPA
CHILDREN

After Sir Edmund Hillary summited Everest with Tenzing Norgay Sherpa he asked how he could help the Sherpa people – a Sherpa friend answered – "our children have eyes, but they are blind and can not see. Therefore, we want you to open their eyes by building a school in our village of Khumjung". Beginning in the 1960s, the Himalayan Trust established schools in several Khumbu villages and foreign aid continues to sponsor young Sherpas both at schools in Khumbu and in Kathmandu. Phinjo Sherpa takes a look at education in Khumbu.

"Education is highly valued by Sherpas and it is shaping the future of Sherpa culture and values, bringing opportunities and challenges. It has opened doors for Sherpa children to pursue careers beyond traditional agriculture or tourism, with many now working in fields like business, medicine, engineering, and tourism management. This shift offers greater economic stability and mobility, allowing young Sherpas to engage with the global economy and improve their families' living conditions.

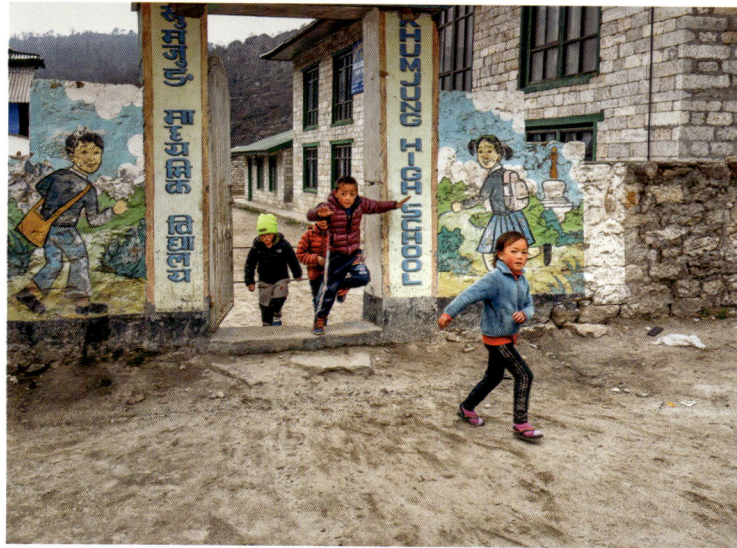

EDUCATION

Access to education has improved significantly, with most Sherpa children now attending school, thanks to the efforts of the government and NGOs. However, remote villages still face challenges with inadequate schooling facilities, and traditional gender roles sometimes limit girls' access to education in more conservative areas.

Most schools in Khumbu teach Nepali and English, enabling students to access global opportunities. However, this push toward education and modern careers can create a generational divide. Schools typically follow Nepal's national curriculum, which emphasises modern subjects, but often lacks representation of Sherpa culture, history, and traditions. This absence can lead to a disconnect from cultural roots. There is concern that, as younger Sherpas focus on formal education and modern lifestyles, traditional practices, festivals, and languages may be neglected. Additionally, the emphasis on written knowledge and Nepali and English languages, risks undermining oral traditions and storytelling that are key elements of Sherpa culture".

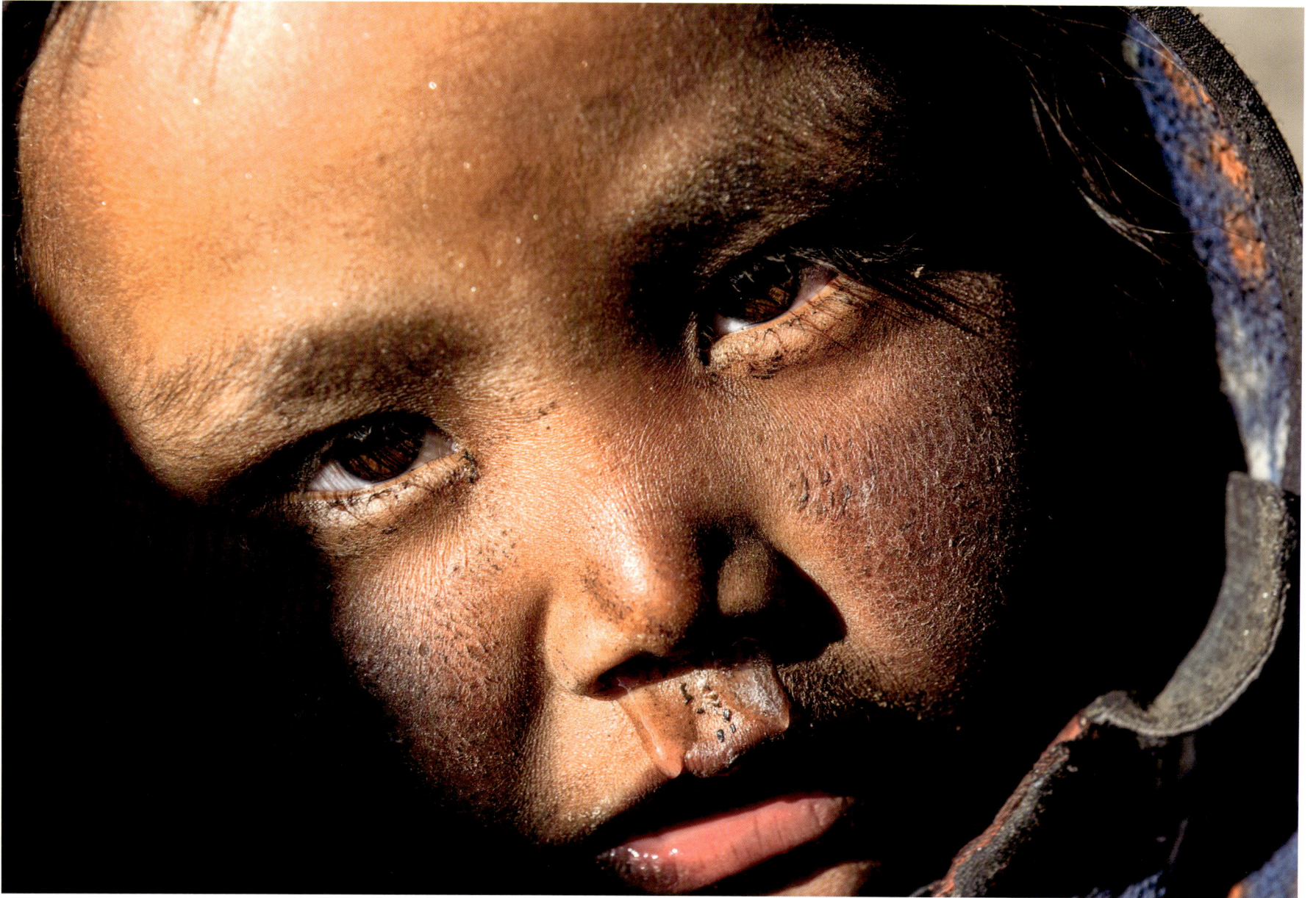

AMAZING PORTERS

Nepalese porters use a head strap (namlo)
to support a basket (doko) and a T-shaped
stick (Tokma) to rest the load on.

There are no roads in Khumbu, so everything that is sold in shops/lodges
and the materials for constructing the shops/lodges has to come from
Kathmandu. The goods usually arrive in Lukla by plane or helicopter and
are then transported on the back of a porter or by yak.

There are three broad and overlapping categories of porters:

Traditional or commercial porters that move goods around Khumbu. They are mostly from the middle hills below Khumbu (Solu) and their loads are generally heavier than trekking porters. Commercial porters earn 65 Rs/kg (2024) from Lukla to Namche, a 100kg load will earn $49 (2024).

Trekking porters carry loads for trekkers and mountaineers up to 30kg, but some may carry double loads, they earn anywhere from $18 to $25 per day (2024).

High altitude porters are mostly Sherpas who carry loads above base camp on mountain expeditions and help clients reach the summit.

The strength and determination of porters has created the myth that porters are superhuman, can carry massive loads in harsh conditions and are used to the cold and high altitudes. The reality is that many porters are farmers from lower down and are as unused to the high altitudes and harsh conditions as trekkers are. So look after them with the same care as all the other members of your trip. To improve the lot of the trek porter, be strict about the weight of loads, the weight limit given by trekking companies is not just to do with excess baggage on planes! Consider every item in your bag because it is going to be carried by a human!

There is the belief among some trekkers that 'unsupported' trekking is laudable, in my opinion this is a misguided view and I believe hiring a porter/guide greatly enhances the enjoyment of the trek and will help the livelihood of one man, his family and village at little extra expense to the trekker.

Community Action Nepal (CAN) run porter rescue shelters in Gokyo, Machermo and Gorak Shep. They also provide free medical care and shelter to porters and trekkers. Responsible trekking agencies provide insurance for their porters and guides, if you are hiring a guide or porter independently, pay for insurance cover as well as their fees and living costs. There are insurance companies in Kathmandu such as www.salico.com.np that will insure guides and porters on an individual basis for a specific time, but it can be time consuming to arrange if you leave it until you get to Nepal.

"What these porters are doing, from our perspective, is sort of unimaginable, even for athletes. In Western society, we no longer have a real handle on what humans can do physically because we're so far removed from this level of daily work that we physically can't do it anymore."

NORMAN HEGLUND MUSCLE

"They start in childhood and adapt over a lifetime. Injuries are rare, probably because they go slowly."

NYINGMA BUDDHISM

Difficult to define, Buddhism began 2,500 years ago in India. It is based on the belief that human life is a cycle of suffering and rebirth. To escape this cycle one must achieve a state of enlightenment (nirvana) through meditation, spiritual study, physical labour and good behaviour. Siddhartha Gautama was the first person to reach enlightenment and became 'The Buddha'.

Buddhists gain merit based on their actions, their attitude to other living beings, participation in ritual and the intentions of their actions. Demonstrating compassion toward sentient beings is particularly beneficial in gaining merit, which determines their level of rebirth, ranging from a hell-bound ghost, a dog, a human to an enlightened being.

Sherpas follow the oldest Tibetan school of buddhism – Nyingma Buddhism. This emphasises mysticism and incorporates shamanistic practices and local gods/spirits borrowed from the pre-buddhist bon religion. They do not recognise a 'traditional' god or gods, but believe that supernatural spirits and demons inhabit the mountains, caves, and forest that help or hinder people on their path towards enlightenment. These spirits and demons must be worshiped/appeased through ancient practices that have become woven into the fabric of Sherpa life. A prominent example is Jomo Miyo Langsangma residing on Chomolungmu, a spirit that is worshiped as the 'Mother of the World'.

There are twenty four Buddhist gompas (monasteries) spread across the Solu-Khumbu with their communities of lamas, monks and nuns who lead a life in isolation searching for enlightenment. They are generally respected and supported by the community, but their contact with the outside world is limited to festivals and the reading of sacred texts at funerals. Day-to-day religious affairs are dealt with by the village lama, who can be married and is often a householder, in addition, shamans and soothsayers deal with the supernatural and the spirit world.

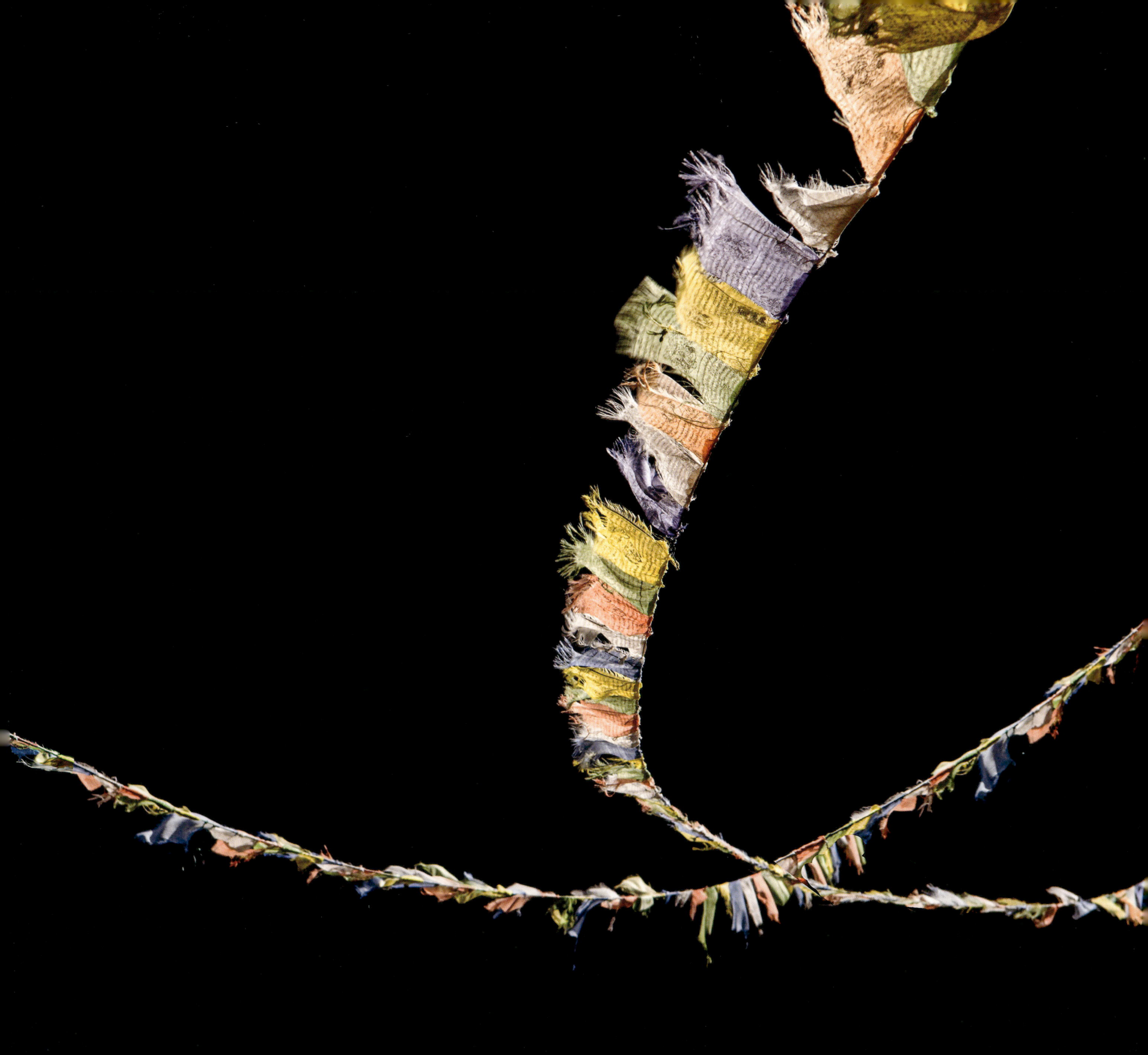

MONKS AND NUNS

Before 1950 schools and medical centres did not exist and gompas were the focus of Sherpa life. There were no mobile phones and Lamas were the only people who could read and write, which meant they had a wide influence on Sherpa society. They made 'lay' rules and established religious festivals and celebrations that were important social gatherings where Sherpas could meet family and friends. For hundreds of years lamas could marry and gompas passed along the family line, but in the middle of the last century some gompas promoted celibacy. This wasn't for prudish, nor spiritual reasons, but because children would make a monastic life problematic. Today, married and unmarried lamas coexist. The various schools and tradition within Buddhism hold different views on women's spiritual attainment, but on the whole they have an equal chance of reaching enlightenment.

The number of Lamas has always varied according to whether the Sherpa population is going through good or bad times.

Phinjo Sherpa explains the current situation.

"As young Sherpas are exposed to education and broader career opportunities in cities or abroad, fewer are interested in monastic life. This decline is linked to broader social, economic, and cultural changes. Traditionally, Sherpa families would send at least one son to become a monk as a way to earn merit and ensure the family's spiritual well-being. However, shrinking family sizes and increasing economic pressures mean fewer families can afford to do so, as children are needed to work and contribute financially.

Monasteries and monks play a crucial role in preserving Sherpa spirituality and culture, deeply rooted in Tibetan Buddhism. With fewer monks, there is a risk of losing important religious knowledge, rituals, and traditions. Monks also provide spiritual guidance and lead key community ceremonies. A significant decline could even lead to monastery closures, which would be a major loss for both the spiritual and cultural heritage of the Khumbu region."

"There's always good and bad parts for everything. But as far as I know, the positive outweighs the negative. It's created a lot of jobs. Tourism is the main industry bringing economic growth to the country. And the Sherpa people appreciate the tourism industry; they always welcome the Western tourists. I mean, there's some kind of changes or influences that we can see. In some places, the culture that we have is kind of disappearing, which is bad; but, learning new things is not bad. As long as you keep your original culture and also learn the new culture, it's good. But sometimes when people learn new things, they forget the old ones... So, I always encourage people, keep what we have, and also learn other culture."

KARMA SHERPA – EVEREST GUIDE

MANI RIMDU
FESTIVAL

Mani Rimdu is a 19-day festival of ceremonies and empowerments, culminating in a 3-day public festival. It's an opportunity for the Sherpa community to celebrate with the monks. Although it is a Sherpa festival, it originated at the Rongphuk Monastery, Tibet, in the early 1900s. It takes place from the first day of the tenth month of the Tibetan lunar calendar, (October/November) at Dawa Choling, Chiwong, and Thame Gompas in Khumbu.

Mani Rimdu is part of the chant of Chenrezig (bodhisattva of compassion and the guiding light of Tibet) and Rimdu are the small red pills that are blessed during the festival. The religious dance (chham) is elaborately choreographed, with monks dressed in colourful costumes and masks. The sixteen Mani dances enact the triumph of Buddhism over the demons of Bon religion and convert symbolic demons into Dharma Protectors. Traditional Tibetan instruments like horns, flutes, cymbals, and drums accompany the ceremonies, engaging body, speech, and mind and act as an offering to the Buddha.

There six important rituals to the festival:

- **Sand Mandala:** Intricate sand art symbolising impermanence. It is surrounded by protective symbols representing the gods.
- **Wong (Empowerment):** Blessings given by the head Lama on the full moon day.
- **Chham (Masked Dance):** Dances symbolising Buddhism's triumph over evil.
- **Ser-Kyem:** Six dancers represent tantric magicians who make offerings of alcohol and tea from silver chalices, and small tormas, to the earth deities.
- **Chhingpa:** Elaborate dances embodying faith and balance, using symbolic masks, movements and tormas (butter-adorned barley flour sculptures) to defend the Buddhist faith.
- **Jinsak (Fire Puja):** An offering to Agni (god of fire) to allay all suffering. Afterwards, the sand mandala is dismantled, and the sand offered to the serpent gods (Nagas).

"Certain movements, sounds, smells, and sight can awaken our psyche and stimulate the states of awareness we describe as gods. The dances are meditations that portray the gods and generate merit for everyone."

TENGBOCHE RINPOCHE

YAKS AND NAKS

“At night and in snowstorms they will protect themselves from the cold by huddling up together with their calves in the warmer centre.”

Yaks a.k.a. Tartary Ox or Grunting Ox are descended from the Wild Ox – bos grunniens. They have evolved to survive in Khumbu and have a similar demeanour to the weather – mostly calm, but sometimes fiery!

They will mostly be seen carrying loads, but they also provide milk, meat, fur, hoof, dung for the fire, fertiliser, bone, skin, tail and clothing. The milk is usually processed into a soft cheese (shomar) spread on potato pancakes or into a dried, hard cheese (churpi). Nak butter is often consumed in salt tea (solcha).

The males are the Yaks and the females are called Naks. Despite their Buddhist faith, Sherpas eat meat and blood, but only from accidental kills or when killed by professional butchers (hyawo). The use of dairy and other products from Nak and crossbreed herds is decreasing as more convenient imported cheese becomes available.

Yak fur is thick black/brown/multihued and occasionally white. They have a thick layer of fat, thick skin with very few sweat glands, a strong rib cage, large muscles, massive lungs and 75% more red blood cells than lowland cattle. Their digestive system is efficient at breaking down low quality food and its tongue and teeth are designed to graze the short grass. These attributes allow them to be comfortable from 2400m to 5500m.

They rarely live beyond twenty years because their teeth wear out! Yaks are often crossbred with cows to create a dzopkyo (male) and dzum (female). These are smaller and do not have the long shaggy hair, but they are happier at lower altitudes and are easier to handle when carrying loads. They are still able to climb in the high hills and carry loads to 5000m. Yaks and crossbreeds continue to be used as pack animals, but their numbers are far fewer than they were a generation ago. Today there are more horses on the EBC trail, but Yaks are better as pack animals because horses are unpredictable and find the ground underfoot difficult on the rough mountain trails.

LODGES

"Eat local foods as much as possible, because imported food items are usually packed in plastic, tin or glass, adding to the volume of waste. We also suggest that trekkers use their own water purifying system or drink boiled water instead of bottled water."

YANGJI DOMA SHERPA

Despite the increase in demand for wood, to be used in cooking, heating and building lodges, there has been minimal deforestation of Khumbu, but the deforestation has shifted to outside the Sagarmatha National Park. Reforestation and conservation initiatives are underway to restore forest cover. Firewood is still used in some villages, but many are shifting to LPG and electricity for cooking and heating. It is not an easy problem to fix – kerosene is expensive and solar heating is slow and unreliable. Solar panels on the roof can reduce wood usage by providing lighting and limited hot water. The communal stove that keeps the lodges warm is less of a worry as it is often powered by yak dung.

So can visitors do anything? First of all eat the same food as the lodge owners rather than 'western' meals. Wash in cold water or wait until you reach a lodge that has solar power rather than using water heated by a wood fire – nobody is going to judge you for not smelling like a rose garden if you've been walking all day. Support the locals efforts by donating to tree-planting organisations, volunteering in reforestation programs and supporting lodges that use non-wood fuels. Trekking outside peak seasons also reduces the strain on resources and infrastructure, distributing the impact of tourism more evenly throughout the year.

TRAILS AND BRIDGES

> "The cables weigh at least 2500kg and are brought in by humans. The men walk one behind the other, securing the weight with a namlo (head strap)."

"I don't have any regrets because I worked very hard indeed to improve the condition for the local people. When we first went in there they didn't have any schools, they didn't have any medical facilities, all over the years we have established 27 schools, we have two hospitals and a dozen medical clinics and then we've built bridges over wild mountain rivers and put in fresh water pipelines so in cooperation with the Sherpas we've done a lot to benefit them."

SIR EDMUND HILLARY, 2003

KHUMBU AT A

It would be easy to romanticise the 'good old days' when fewer people visited and travellers stayed with the locals, but overlooking the positive impacts of tourism on Sherpa communities would be shortsighted. Phinjo Sherpa reflects on the complexities that modern tourism has brought to Khumbu.

"Tourism has greatly transformed Sherpa lives, many now work as guides, lodge owners, or trekking operators, earning far more than traditional farming and herding ever provided. Living standards have improved, with better housing, healthcare, education, and infrastructure. The money from tourism has also supported cultural preservation, with local entrepreneurs and NGOs helping to restore monasteries and uphold ancient rituals. Tourism has had another upside in that it has fostered pride in Sherpa heritage and opened doors to cross cultural exchange and global connections.

However, tourism has brought change and traditional values are shifting. The focus on family, community, and religion is waning, with younger Sherpas drawn to tourism's financial rewards over traditional livelihoods, resulting in some generational divides. Western goods and ideas are reshaping Sherpa identity, and there's a concern that materialism and individualism may erode cultural values, language, and Buddhist beliefs. Education, while valuable, is contributing to a "brain drain," as young Sherpas that study abroad often don't return, this slows local progress.

Environmental challenges add to this strain on Sherpa life. Climate change threatens agriculture and tourism (see page page 24), while waste from tourism pollutes rivers and land, and a decline in the number of visitors creates economic vulnerabilities for Sherpas that have taken out loans.

Despite these challenges, younger Sherpas are aware of the importance of their heritage and actively try to balance modern life with cultural traditions, seeing

CROSS ROADS

"sustainable" tourism as a way forward. This means combining eco-friendly practices with respect for the community, they hope to protect Sherpa heritage and create a sustainable future for Khumbu."

Lhakpa Sherpa looks further at the impact of tourism on Khumbu.

"Before the rise of modern tourism, Khumbu's economy was a balance of small-scale tourism, farming, animal husbandry, and trading salt with Tibet. However, when China closed the Nangpa La, the salt trade ended, coinciding with a tourism boom that proved more profitable than following traditional practices. This shift has contributed to a decline in Sherpa knowledge, language, and culture, while the increasing number of visitors has disrupted local wildlife, driving away species like musk deer, impeyan pheasants, and Tibetan snow cocks.

The unregulated building of lodges has reduced job opportunities across the community, because camping requires more labour than lodges. As a result, economic inequality has widened, with those in prime locations profiting, while others struggle.

Helicopters are a modern concern. Frequent flights out of Gorak Shep, Pheriche, and Dingboche only benefit helicopter companies and cut into local income. They also create noise pollution, further disturbing wildlife. Unregulated flights need to be controlled to prevent potential conflict with locals.

Khumbu stands at a crossroads. Now is the time to improve lodge standards, reduce helicopter flights, encourage responsible tourism, offer hygienic local food, and organise treks to support the entire community, from porters to guides, while protecting the environment."

"Although we touched each place for only a day and then moved on, I wondered how many such passings could be made before the imprint would become indelible."

TOM HORNBEIM, 1963 AMERICAN EVEREST EXPEDITION

The locals of Khumjung and Thame have preserved Sherpa culture through language, festivals, costumes, and way of life, which will be lost soon if it is not preserved. They see tourism as a positive force to preserve their culture.

"...we would like the world to know that Sherpa culture has not disappeared which will help restore and preserve the Sherpa culture..."

ONGCHU

KANI, STUPA, PRAYER FLAGS AND MANI STONES

As you wander through Khumbu you will come across many physical manifestations of Buddhism, but what are they?

Kani are archways marking the entrances to villages, painted with images of Buddhist deities and intricate mandalas, which represent the Buddhist cosmos. These colourful gateways welcome visitors and create a sense of spiritual protection for the village.

Stupas (Chortens), originating in India, are built to bring blessings to the local area and to all who pass by. Traditionally, Stupas housed relics of the Buddha; modern ones often contain sacred objects like prayer scrolls, jewellery, or other valuable (though not always expensive) items. A unique element within the stupa is the 'Tree of Life,' a wooden pole wrapped in gems and inscribed with thousands of mantras. During a special ceremony, people hold colourful ribbons connected to the 'Tree of Life' to make wishes, infusing the stupa with energy. Eyes are often painted on the upper portion of the stupa gazing in four directions to symbolise the Buddha's all-seeing awareness.

Prayer flags, or Lungdar, flutter from homes, mountain passes, and sacred sites. Each colour has symbolic meaning: blue for the sky, white for air or wind, red for fire, green for water, and yellow for earth. Printed with images and Buddhist teachings, these flags often feature a Lungta (wind horse) at the center, a symbol of speed and the transformation of bad fortune into good. In the corners, you may see the four sacred animals — the dragon, garuda (mythical bird), tiger, and snow lion. These flags are also covered with mantras and prayers for the person who raised them. As the wind passes through, it carries the blessings, goodwill, and compassion across the landscape. When the flags fade, it's believed the prayers have become part of the universe, and new flags are raised in their place.

Mani stones are flat slabs inscribed with the mantra of Avalokiteshvara, "Om mani padme hum," and are often stacked into walls. Tradition holds that these mani walls should be passed on the left side in a clockwise direction, aligning with the rotation of the world, to show respect and devotion.

LUKLA **2846m**
TENZING HILLARY
AIRPORT

Perched on a mountainside surrounded by steep mountains, with a wall at one end and at the other a steep drop into the valley, is 'the most dangerous airport in the world'. Sir Edmund Hillary bought the land from local Sherpas for $2650 and in 1964, Lukla airport was born, but did not operate until 1971. It is rumoured that Hillary bought some alcohol and got the locals to perform a foot stomping dance to flatten the land as a runway – the tarmac came in 2001.

Once an aircraft starts its approach, there are no second chances! At altitude, the lower air density reduces the power generated by the engines, thereby lowering lift and making it more challenging to slow the plane. The runway is only 527m, which is very short,

international airports are often more than 3048m! To help planes slow down on landing and accelerate on take off, the runway slopes with a gradient of 12%.

The airport can only handle helicopters and small aircraft such as Pilatus PC-6 Turbo Porters, DHC-6 Twin Otters and Dornier Do 228s.

The label as dangerous is much less relevant today because Nepal's Civil Aviation Authority sets high standards for pilots wanting to fly into Lukla. They must complete 100 short take off and landing flights, have at least one year's experience in Nepal and have successfully completed ten flights with a certified instructor.

HOME TOWN OF SHERPAS

Tourism started in the early 1950s, but it wasn't until 1967 that the first tourist shop opened and the first Sherpa lodge was established in 1971. Since then the number of shops and lodges has increased exponentially, with Namche Bazaar now a bustling settlement with all the 'best' amenities and facilities for tourists.

Namche has an internet café, bakery, Irish pub, rooms with attached bathrooms, hot showers, mountain wear, local handicraft shops, television with international channels and even karaoke to live up to the changes brought about by tourism.

Increasingly important is the Sherpa Cultural Museum at Sherwi Khangba lodge, set up by Lhakpa Sonam Sherpa to help preserve the history and culture of the region. Namche also has monasteries, stupas, and a local market where the people from the lower valley come to trade, no longer using cheese and butter, but now in exchange for money.

DAWA CHOLING GOMPA 3867m

Way above the meeting of the Dudh Kosi and Imja Khola rivers is the beautiful Dawa Choling Gompa or Tengboche Monastery. Lama Sangwa Dorje (founder of the oldest monastery at Pangboche) prophesised that there would be monastery built here. There is an imprint of his foot that he left in a rock while meditating, it can be seen at the entrance to Dawa Choling. Some of the temples, chortens and smaller religious shrines are from 1880, but the monastery was built much later between 1916 and 1919, during Ngawang Tenzin Norbu's time. Norbu was Sangwa Dorje's fifth incarnation and he blessed Chatang Chotar (Lama Gulu) to found the monastery.

It is the largest gompa in Khumbu with 50/60 monks. The founding of the gompa was important because it showed that Khumbu was a proper Buddhist community, capable of funding its construction and maintenance, the commissioning of paintings and statues, and securing numerous sacred texts from Tibet. Three wealthy Sherpas are credited with funding the monastery. The strength of Khumbu as a Buddhist community is also shown by the fact that it could provide enough food and tea for each monk and further by the sacrifice of family members to the monastery who would otherwise be helping the family.

The early monastery was unfortunately destroyed during an earthquake in 1934. Lama Gulu's successor, Umze Gelden, with monks, locals and a skilled carpenter from Lhasa in Tibet re-established the monastery.

Bad luck struck again in 1989 when the monastery's precious old scriptures, statues, murals and wood carvings were destroyed in a devastating fire caused by an electrical short circuit. Following the fire, funds from around the world helped Nawang Tenzing Jangpo (the incarnation of Lama Gulu) to rebuild it.

Contributions from around the world have also created a clean water supply, a small hydropower station, a high altitude medicinal herb plantation, an eco-centre, better toilets and accommodation for porters.

"Tengboche must be one of the most beautiful places in the world. The height is well over 12,000 feet. The Monastery buildings stand upon a knoll at the end of a big spur, which is flung out across the direct axis of the Imja river. Surrounded by satellite dwellings, all quaintly constructed and oddly mediaeval in appearance, it provides a grandstand beyond comparison for the finest mountain scenery that I have ever seen, whether in the Himalaya or elsewhere."

JOHN HUNT, LEADER OF THE SUCCESSFUL EVEREST EXPEDITION

THE DEBOCHE NUNNERY

Nuns studied and practiced Buddhism at the Tengboche Monastery right from the start, but after a few years the nuns needed an exclusive place to live and pray. In 1925, the head of the monastery, Lama Gulu, gave them land in Deboche a small valley below the monastery and they built a nunnery and monastery. Since 2005 it has been under repair, but in 2015 an almost brand new nunnery was built with help from many groups.

BUDDHIST BOOKS

There were no books when Siddhartha Gautama – the founder of Buddhism and the first "Buddha" or enlightened one – lived 2,500 years ago. It took 400 years before his disciples wrote about his teachings in Sanskrit and Pali languages then later they were translated into Tibetan.

The *Ka-gyur* and the *Ten-gyur are the most important collections*. The *Ka- gyur* (108 volumes) records the Buddha's teachings. *Ka* means Buddha's word and *gyur* means translated.

The *Ten-gyur* (226 volumes) are commentaries on the *Ka-gyur* written by Buddha's followers. It is believed that there are about 8 *Ten-gyur* in the Solukhumbu.

All the monasteries have a collection of these books. There are also other books for home use: *Boom* – 16 books with 100,000 verses of Buddha's thoughts and *Domang* – a single book with an extract from the most important parts of the *Ka-gyur*.

AMA DABLAM
6812m

Sitting above the village of Pangboche is an iconic mountain – Ama Dablam – 'Matterhorn' of Khumbu. It is one of the most striking mountains on earth, dominating the skyline during the majority of the trek to EBC. Ama Dablam means – 'mother and her necklace'. The hanging glacier below the summit is the 'dablam', a traditional double pendant worn by Sherpa women that contains pictures of their gods and the peak's long ridges resemble the arms of a mother/grandmother or the world – 'Ama' – protecting her child.

CLIMBING AMA DABLAM

Sir Edmund Hillary described it as "beautiful, but unclimbable", always a 'red rag' to climbers, it was first climbed in 1961 by Mike Gill (NZ), Barry Bishop (USA), Mike Ward (UK) and Wally Romanes (NZ) via the Southwest Ridge. This is still the safest and most popular route for commercial companies with 2/3 camps after base camp. It is protected by a plethora of fixed ropes and to climb it you need to be comfortable jumaring on steep rock whilst carrying a big rucsack, scrambling on narrow ridges and front pointing on steep ice.

"Climbing is all about facing the unknown and the outcome should remain uncertain until the end."

DOUG SCOTT

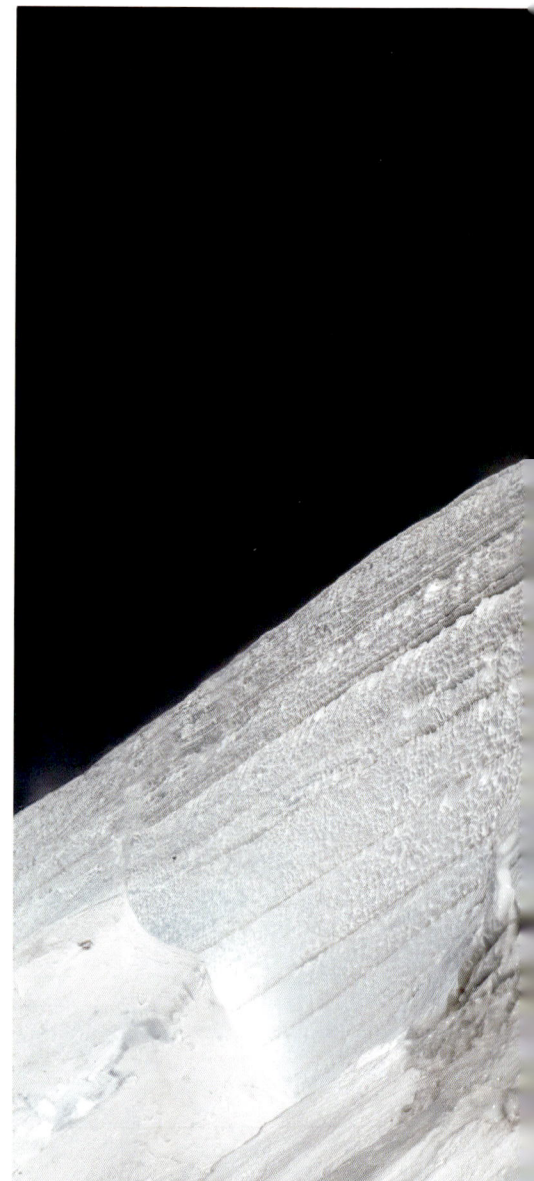

"I have done many periods of solitary mediation. Sometimes I will spend months at a time mediating and during these periods I see no other people. When I meditate at the nunnery, I sit here and look across the valley to Ama Dablam. When I do this, everything I know fades away and the only focus of my mind is the mountain. Everest is just a mountain, but Ama Dablam is a place I have a spiritual connection with. But the gods live on the summits of all the mountains. There's no spiritual gain from climbing the mountains. People do it only for money. I don't like that people climb the mountains, but people need to earn money and maybe if you're poor and have no other way of earning money – like for many of the Sherpa climbers here – then the gods can forgive you. For the foreigners, though, it's different. I don't know if the gods forgive them for climbing to the summits."

MINGMA PHUTI – PANGBOCHE NUN

DINGBOCHE

4400m

A few hours further along the trail than Pangboche is a sunny and sheltered village facing the formidable north ridge of Ama Dablam. It is situated at the start of the Imja Khosi valley just after the main valley forks – to the north is the route to EBC and to the east is the trail to Chukhung and Imje Tse (Island Peak). It is surrounded by small fields, enclosed by stone walls, that are for the cultivation of potatoes, buckwheat and grass to feed Yaks. The first Sherpas believed that Tibetan barley could only grow using water from the Imja river that flowed through Dingboche. However, since 2015 many of the fields have had lodges built on them, are used to grow potatoes or simply deserted and barley isn't grown anymore.

It has a small 'year round' population of around seventy people, although this is considerably more during the tourist season. Most trekkers spend a day or two resting and acclimatising at Dingboche by ascending the hiking peak – Nangkartshang (Nangkar Peak) above the village.

DOLMA RI / POKALDE PEAK 5806m

This is possibly the shortest and easiest 'trekking peak' in Khumbu. It is quite exposed in places and very steep involving some easy scrambling near the top. The approach is from Chukhung and part way up the route leading to the Kongma La.

The first ascent was made in April 1953 by the Everest Expedition team led by John Hunt. They ascended it from the Kongma La (5535m) along its north ridge.

CHUKHUNG 4730m

Chukhung is a small village further along the the Imja Khola valley. It is directly below the Kongma La and gives access to Dolma Ri and Chukhung Ri. The latter is a small trekking peak with no technical climbing and is used as an acclimatisation peak for those going onto Imja Tse or over the Kongma La. From the summit of Chukhung Ri there are fantastic views of Imja Tse, Ama Dablam, Makalu, and the south face of Nuptse.

CHUKHUNG RI 5546m

"I love to sit on a mountain top and gaze. I don't think of
anything but the people I care about and the view."

JULIAN LENNON

IMJA TSE /
ISLAND PEAK

6160m

Named Island Peak in 1951 by Eric Shipton's party because it appears as an island in a sea of ice when viewed from Dingboche it is actually an extension of the ridge coming down off the south end of Lhotse Shar.

In 1983, it was renamed Imja Tse, but Island Peak remains popular all over the world.

It was first climbed in 1953 by C.Evans, A.Gregory, C.Wylie, T.Norgay, plus seven other Sherpas.

TO LOBUCHE ALONG THE KHUMBU KHOLA VALLEY

The Khumbu Glacier melts into
the Lobujya (Lobuche) River

DHUGLA AND TSUKPU LHARA

4620m

At the far end of the broad Khumbu Khola valley and south of the Khumbu Glacier is Dhugla, a small hamlet of buildings. It is not inhabited all year and is essentially a collection of lodges used by some trekkers as an intermediate stop en route to Lobuche and EBC.

Above Dhugla is Tsukpu Lhara – a memorial ground for some of the people who died attempting to climb Mt Everest and other peaks. There there are cairns, prayer flags, and memorials over a wide flat area.

LOBUJE / LOBUCHE

4940m

Lobuje is a small hamlet en route to Everest Base Camp with a variety
of basic accommodation and a bakery/cafe.

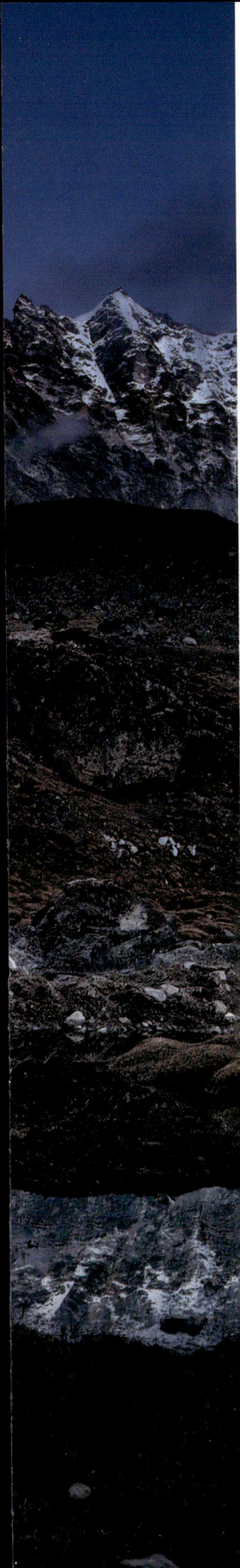

LOBUJE / LOBUCHE EAST

6119m

Lobuje East is the Eastern peak of Lobuje peak. The high camp is a four hour hike from the village of Lobuche. The first ascent of Lobuche East was made by Laurence Nielson and Sherpa Ang Gyalzen on April 25, 1984. The SE ridge is the most popular and is graded PD+.

NAMCHE BAZAAR TO LUNGDEN ALONG THE BHOTE KHOSI VALLEY

"I look at climbing not so much as standing on the top as seeing the other side. There are always other horizons in front of you, other horizons to go beyond."

SIR CHRIS BONINGTON

CROSSING THE RENJO LA 5460m

"I was lucky today, I woke up and am alive,
I have this precious life and I will not waste it."

BUDDHIST PHILOSOPHY

TO GOKYO

4750m

Gokyo is one of the highest villages in the world. It used to be a summer yak holding settlement, but is now a trekking destination. Named after Gokyo Ri (5357m) – a peak rising directly above the village – it has the world's highest freshwater lake system, partially fed by the Ngozumpa glacier, which descends from the world's 6th highest mountain – Cho Oyo.

There are six lakes, forming a unique wetland, the one closest to Gokyo – Thonak lake – is the largest and is where 'Nag Devata', the Hindu snake God lives. A temple of the Hindu deities Vishnu and Shiva is situated at the western corner of the lake. During the Janai Purnima festival 500+ Hindus visit to bathe in the lake.

On average 7000 tourists visit Gokyo and the lakes each year, which means that nearly all the buildings are now guest houses. This causes a problem for the lake – human waste! Western tourists expect flushing toilets, showers and other facilities, the traditional compost toilet that used to provide manure for the fields has been replaced with septic tanks, where the overflow feeds directly into the main lake – "killing the goose that lays the golden eggs" comes to mind.

"...In my view it is not just about the mountain, I think that's what inspired Sir Edmund Hillary too, you know. He not only promoted Everest but the people as well. Later in between, we lost that touch. And we started promoting Everest rather than the whole Khumbu..."

CHO OYO   8188m

TO DZONGLA

4830m

Dzongla is a small settlement at the head of the Khumbu Khola valley and is the gateway to the Cho La

DZONGLA **4830m**

CROSSING THE CHO LA TO DRAGNAG

CROSSING THE KONGMA LA **5535m**

The Kongma La is the easternmost pass of the 'Three Passes Trek' and links Lobuche with Chukhung by first crossing the Khumbu Glacier. It is considered the most difficult of the Three Passes Trek – Renjo La, Cho La and Kongma La. It can be done anticlockwise or clockwise

A kongma is a species of mountain pheasant that live in Khumbu.

PUMO RI 7161m

Sometimes written as Pumori it combines the sherpa words Pumo, for a young, unmarried daughter, and Ri for "mountain". It was first climbed via the southeast ridge during May 1962 by Gerhard Lenser on a German/Swiss expedition. It has become the 'classic route' with three camps. The mountain's worst moment came during the 2015 earthquake when a large part of Pumori's ridge collapsed, triggering a monster avalanche that reached EBC killing 22 people.

GORAK SHEP

5164m

Gorak shep is the final stop on most trekkers route to Everest Base Camp as their trekking permits do not allow them to stop at EBC.

Gorak Shep was the original Everest Base Camp, used by the Swiss Expedition in 1952, but it was later moved closer to the Khumbu Ice Fall.

Gorak Shep means 'dead Ravens' because of the complete lack of vegetation in the area.

EVEREST BASE CAMP – EBC

Every Spring the head of the Khumbu glacier changes into EBC from a blank glacier to a 'tented city' with up to 1500 people. During a 2 to 3 month period, hundreds of mountaineers congregate to ascend Everest with their Sherpa guides.

The 'Ghorkha' earthquake

In 2015 the worst earthquake to hit Nepal in eighty years killed 9000 people and injured many more. Because it was only nine miles deep, the first quake caused a lot of shaking near the surface. Poorly constructed multi-story brick buildings and temples in and around Kathmandu were reduced to rubble. Khumbu villages with their poor infrastructure and houses made of stacked stones or timbers and mud were destroyed by landslides, avalanches, and shaking. The earthquake destroyed almost half the schools in Khumbu, 40% of the population had their houses fully destroyed and 42% partially destroyed. Thame was almost completely destroyed!

Today the physical scars are hidden, but many Sherpa families still carry the burden of the loss of family members, but Khumbu's strong sense of community has helped them to rebuild quickly.

The earthquake also triggered several large avalanches on and around Chomolungmu. One originating on nearby Pumori swept through Everest Base Camp killing 22 people (10 sherpas) and stranded more in high camps on the mountain. Teams tried to repair the route through the icefall, but another avalanche took out most of the ladders and killed three more sherpas. The stranded climbers were eventually brought down by helicopter.

The Khumbu Glacier

The Khumbu glacier is the largest and highest glacier in Nepal. It starts at the head of the 'Western Cwm' 7600m between Mount Everest and the Lhotse-Nuptse ridge and runs down to 4900m. The Khumbu Glacier moves approximately 0.9 to 1.2m down the flank of Mt Everest every day. Ice entering the icefall takes approximately 4.3 years to emerge at the base, which is 600m lower and one linear mile away!

In the '90s, commercial guiding Nepal boomed and today, base camp bustles with helicopters and offers high-speed Wi-Fi. It is an enormous camp catering for up to 1500 climbers. The growth of the camp is unregulated and the government are concerned that it poses a threat to the already fragile environment.

"With the boom of commercial mountaineering, people have forgotten the essence of the mountain deities, there are so many people climbing these mountains, living on the glaciers, and the waste they produce is polluting the sanctity of these sacred landforms."

KANCHHA SHERPA – 1953 EVEREST ASCENT TEAM

Puja

Everest Base Camp and the mountains are considered holy and a local lama performs puja at an alter created by the Sherpas. Puja – the act of showing reverence to a god or spirit – is a very colourful and joyful celebration, a ritual cleansing of evil, bad luck or bad karma. It is performed by a lama who can read ancient Tibetan script and can last hours as offerings of food, drink, prayer flags, khatas (scarfs) and climbing equipment are blessed. The puja moves through many stages asking for forgiveness for the damage caused by the climbers and safety for all.

Burning juniper and incense represents good luck and purification of the area. Rice and flour are thrown into the air, which is meant to draw attention to the puja. At the end of the ceremony a bowl of tsampa (rice or roasted barley flour) is passed round and people smear the rice paste on each others faces to represent good luck and acts as a welcome.

CHOMOLUNGMU 8848m

Discovery of the highest mountain on earth

In 1849, British surveyor James Nicholson aimed his theodolite at a distant peak, then known only as "b" (later designated Peak XV). British cartographers were meticulous about preserving local names, but with so many variations, in 1865 the Surveyor General Andrew Waugh chose to rename it "Mount Everest" in honour of his predecessor, Sir George Everest. At that time, the peak's height was unknown, so this naming wasn't the grand gesture it might seem today — just a practical solution for an unnamed mountain. A few years later, Radhanath Sikdar, a "computer" working for the British Survey from an officc in India, used his expertise in trigonometry to calculate that Peak XV was indeed the tallest mountain on earth, initially measured at 8840m, later revised to 8848m. Ironically, George Everest himself had never seen the mountain; he just happened to be in the right place at the right time to lend his name to what would become the world's most famous peak. And, interestingly, we all mispronounce it: Sir George Everest pronounced his name "Eve-rest," not "Ev-er-est."

Locally, the Sherpa people call it Chomolungmu (or Quomolungma or Jomolungma), a name that comes from the goddess Jomo Miyo Langsangma, meaning "Goddess Mother of the World." Nepal didn't have an official name for it until 1956, when it was called Sagarmatha, or "Forehead of the Sky."

It took 101 years, the lives of 24 climbers, and fifteen expeditions before a British team led by Lord Hunt reached the summit in 1953, with New Zealander Edmund Hillary and Sherpa Tenzing Norgay making the final ascent. Sadly, the names of the many who attempted the climb before them often go unremembered, such as Tom Bourdillon and Charles Evans, who paved the way and reached within 90 metres of the summit just a day earlier, only to be forced back by failing oxygen equipment.

An elite team of Sherpa guides called 'the icefall doctors' work together to fix ropes and ladders from base camp to the top. Without them nobody would reach the summit. Sherpas also stock camps with tents, stoves, bottled oxygen, and food. They then support their clients to the summit.

There are many detractors about ascents on Everest, but every mountaineer knows that given then chance they would try to climb it, because it is without doubt a beautiful route and a wonderful mountain.

Most attempts to climb Chomolungmu are made during May just as the monsoon season approaches. The jet stream, an area of high wind that typically sits on the summit, then moves north, improving the conditions for climbing. There are 17 different routes to the top of Everest, but most mountaineers use the first ascent line – the southeast ridge or south col route. Every year hundreds reach the summit aided by the infrastructure from commercial expeditions, built on the backs of Sherpas. The total number as of 2023 was 6664 people have reached the top with some having done it multiple times — Kami Rita Sherpa has climbed it 29 times!

"Other mountains share with Everest a history
of adventure, glory, and tragedy, but only
Everest is the highest place on earth."

WILLIAM SIRI

"Climb if you will, but remember that courage and strength are nought without prudence, and that a momentary negligence may destroy the happiness of a lifetime. Do nothing in haste; look well to each step; and from the beginning think what may be the end."

EDWARD WHYMPER

"People ask me, 'What is the use of climbing Mount Everest?' and my answer must at once be, 'It is of no use.' There is not the slightest prospect of any gain whatsoever. Oh, we may learn a little about the behaviour of the human body at high altitudes... and possibly medical men may turn our observation to some account for the purposes of aviation. But otherwise nothing will come of it. We shall not bring back a single bit of gold or silver, not a gem, nor any coal or iron... If you cannot understand that there is something in man which responds to the challenge of this mountain and goes out to meet it, that the struggle is the struggle of life itself upward and forever upward, then you won't see why we go. What we get from this adventure is just sheer joy. And joy is, after all, the end of life. We do not live to eat and make money. We eat and make money to be able to live. That is what life means and what life is for."

GEORGE MALLORY

The Khumbu Icefall

"In my experience, to climb Everest, people have to have some sort of mountaineering skills. But physical strength is more important than technical training... I mean, climbing on Everest is also about luck. The person has to have good luck. No matter who you are, sometimes it is not easy to get on the summit. A lot of things must come together – weather, physical body condition, guiding."

KARMA SHERPA – EVEREST GUIDE

The 'icefall doctors' make climbing Chomolungmu possible

Climbers ascending Chomolungmu from the Khumbu side will cross more than 200 crevasses in their acclimatisation rotations and ascend many steep ice walls. This is done mostly via ladders and ropes put in place by a dedicated Sherpa team called the 'Icefall Doctors' whose responsibility is to maintain the fixed ropes and ladders to Camp I and beyond.

The 'Icefall Doctors' are selected and paid for by the Sagarmatha Pollution Control Committee (SPCC). Since 1977, the SPCC has been responsible for the route through the icefall and each expedition member pays for the icefall doctors. It is a dangerous and demanding job and without the 'Icefall Doctors' few climbers on commercial expeditions would reach the summit.

The ladders can be single or multiple three, four or even five strapped together, the longer they are the more bounce there is. The climber clips into a 'safety line" and leans forward using the lines as tension. If they are fortunate to have feet the correct size, their crampons fit neatly across the rungs, but if they are too short or too long the process becomes trickier.

> "I don't want to pretend that Sherpas have somehow been shortchanged because I don't believe it. They are guns for hire, and they do it for money not fame. If a western climber wants to pretend to him or herself that they climbed Everest fair and square when someone was carrying their gear or short-roping them, they lose, no one else."

ED DOUGLAS

The Curse of the 8000m Mountain

Tom Livingstone wrote about the "curse of the 8000m mountain" after an attempt on Gasherbrum IV a 7925m mountain that has only had a handful of ascents.

"We're the only team on the mountain, (Gasherbrum IV, 7925m) whereas nearby Gasherbrum 2 (8035m) has had about 30 people on it, and K2 (8611m) has reportedly seen 100 people summit via the standard route. This is the 'curse' of an 8000 metre mountain. It's distressing to see this side of peak-bagging: no care for the mountain, just oxygen, Sherpas, fixed ropes, piles of trash, radios, satellite connections, complete inexperience, a massive dependency on others and their hard work, helicopters, money, 'speed records,' selfies, and accidents. I shake my head and walk away. This scene bares no resemblance to mountaineering, alpinism, or climbing."

TOM LIVINGSTON

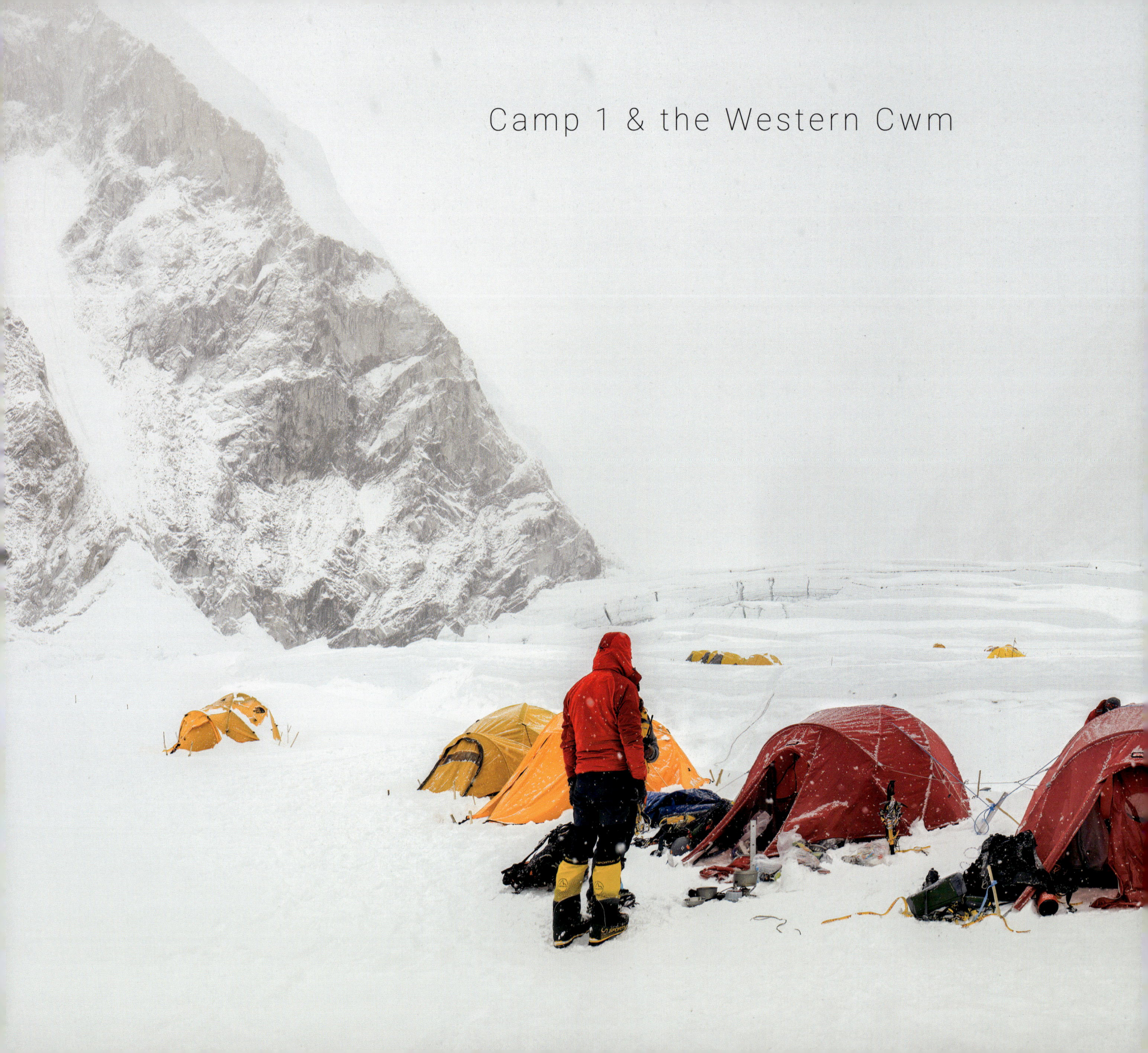
Camp 1 & the Western Cwm

Altitude

As altitude increases, oxygen molecules are spaced further apart and each breath contains fewer oxygen molecules than at sea level. To compensate, the rate and depth of breathing increase, and the heart works faster and harder to circulate oxygen throughout the body. The good news is the body can adapt by producing more red blood cells and haemoglobin, it also increases urination to removes excess bicarbonates and fluid from the blood. Everyone adapts at their own rate regardless of fitness. On the EBC trek, 40% of trekkers experience Acute Mountain Sickness (AMS), but it is rare for it to progress to the potentially fatal high-altitude pulmonary oedema (HAPE) and high-altitude cerebral oedema (HACE). The only way to know how you'll react to altitude is by experiencing it, and understanding the symptoms.

The symptoms of AMS are similar to a hangover and can be mild or severe. Ascending too quickly and having a genetic predisposition, influence whether you will experience AMS. The trick is to let your body gradually get used to the increasing altitude – this varies from person to person; what is gradual for one person may be too quick for another. If you develop AMS and it hasn't reduced or disappeared overnight with pain killers and anti-inflammatory medicine, do not go higher. If you do not improve or symptoms worsen over 24 to 48 hours descend to where you feel better. It doesn't necessarily require a helicopter, just go down.

To reduce the risk of AMS
- Go slowly, particularly if feeling unwell.
- Ideally, increase the altitude you sleep at by no more than 300 to 500m per day.
- Stay hydrated, but know that hydration alone doesn't prevent altitude sickness; drink according to thirst, without forcing yourself to drink.
- Eat adequately, and minimise alcohol and smoking.
- If you drink caffeine regularly keep drinking it because stopping suddenly can cause symptoms similar to AMS.

The medication Diamox (Acetazolamide) can reduce the likelihood of AMS with minimal side effects. If you're concerned about AMS, consult a knowledgeable doctor experienced in prescribing Diamox for altitude adaptation.

Crevasses

Crevasses can form as the glacier moves over undulations in the ground below. They form mainly in the top 50m where the ice is more brittle, below that the ice is more flexible and can slide over uneven surfaces without cracking. They also form when sections of a glacier move at different speeds. e.g. the glacier moves faster in the middle yet slower on the sides as it scrapes against the valley walls.

Camp 2

Camp 3 and the summit

"Everest is the reason this area exists at all. The whole financial existence of the valley depends on Everest and the other big mountains. For me, Everest doesn't have any spiritual significance, but it does have financial and business significance."

TSHETEN DORJE SHERPA

"I looked up to my right and forty feet above me was a rounded snow cone. A few blows of the ice axe, a few weary steps and I was on the top. My first reaction was that of relief."

SIR EDMUND HILLARY

The 'Pocket Rocket' on Everest

"A childhood obsession to climb the world's highest peak – Everest, eventually led me to reality, and on May 23rd 2008, as this mighty mountain cast her dawn shadow over the Western Cwm and surrounding Himalayan peaks a dream came true for myself and my client.

After several weeks of gruelling preparation and acclimatisation we were ready for our summit attempt. As ever the Khumbu ice fall with its teetering blocks of ice and avalanches made our hearts race even more than the altitude. The relief of reaching the beautiful Western Cwm and the safety of Camp 2 allowed our bodies to relax momentarily. Climbing the steep slopes of the Lhotse Face was delightful and the sun warmed our chilled bodies as we clambered into our tent perched on an icy ledge at just over 7000m. After resting our bodies and minds the easier traverse across to the yellow band revealed the pure beauty of the mountain. At the South Col our trustworthy Sherpa's smiles were enough to comfort us in this inhospitable place. Internally we contained our fear and excitement and at 9pm, with our Sherpa's close by, we departed for the summit.

After many hours slowly creeping upwards along exposed ridges we were standing on top of the world. Few words were spoken as we took in where we were and silently gazed into the distance at the outstanding majestic views.

After 30 minutes on the top, with tattered nerves and extremely tired, but very much in control, we descended first to the South Col and then back to base camp to be greeted by our Sirdar; it was only then that the tears of relief and joy began to flow.

15 years on climbing Everest is still in the forefront of my mind and fills me with an internal satisfying glow."

ADELE PENNINGTON

Adele Pennington is the first British woman to have climbed Everest twice. The first British female winter ascent of Ama Dablam She holds the British female record for climbing six 8000m peaks.

THE PROBLEM
OF HELICOPTERS
IN KHUMBU

Helicopter flights have been an issue for many a year as expedition and trekking operators increasingly use helicopters to transport mountaineers and hikers into and out of Sagarmatha National Park, even EBC.

The use of helicopters beyond Lukla has negatively affected the forest, environment and wildlife. The constant noise from helicopters has directly impacted local residents and trekkers.

Furthermore, this has an impact on lodge owners, yak owners and porters that are missing out on important income.

There has also been a web of unethical practices and financial exploitation when calling helicopters for rescue. The rise in helicopter rescues from 70 per 100k trekkers in 1988 to 3500 per 100k trekkers in 2018 is alarming, especially when the number of actual fatalities due to Acute Mountain Sickness (AMS) has remained relatively constant.

The core of this scam involves unscrupulous trekking companies/guides, helicopter operators, and medical providers encouraging trekkers with mild symptoms of AMS to opt for helicopter rescue rather than descending to lower altitude. They do this in exchange for 'kickbacks' from helicopter companies and/or hospitals. In some ugly cases, lazy trekkers pretend to be sick to take a helicopter. The scam is further exacerbated by low budget trekking companies pushing trekkers to ascend too quickly, even using laxatives to deliberately dehydrate them, a particularly concerning and dangerous part of the scam.

The financial impact of these scams affects insurance companies, which have to cover costs, and trekkers who see their insurance premiums rise, or worse, can't get insurance. Some insurance companies have responded by requiring pre-approval for rescues, which can cause issues where immediate action is required.

To address this problem the Khumbu Pasang lhamu Rural Municipality has announced that commercial helicopter flights will be prohibited in the national park from January 2025. Only rescue flights will be permitted, and these must be coordinated with the national park authority. However, this has been tried in 2023 and 2024 with limited effect, you don't have be a prophet to predict that commercial companies will beat environmental protection and the well being of locals.

The absence of strict enforcement means the onus falls on trekkers to be more informed when booking treks. Trekking companies offering extremely cheap packages may be more likely to engage in fraudulent activities to make up the costs.

Trekkers should learn about AMS, its symptoms, what to do when experiencing altitude sickness and realise that most cases can be managed by descending on foot.

Insurers must require robust documentation of the rescue - detailed medical reports, interviews with all involved parties and cross-checking of accounts to identify fraud.

Nepal's government should instigate rigid checks, use GPS tracking of helicopters, request clear documentation of the medical need for a rescue and impose heavy fines or bans on companies and individuals.

One possible solution could be for a local Nepalese insurance company to handle helicopter insurance, instead of relying on international insurers. This would localise the system, making it easier to monitor and potentially reduce fraud.

"When we respect our environment, we respect ourselves."

GYALWANG DRUKPA

KATHMANDU
GATEWAY TO KHUMBU

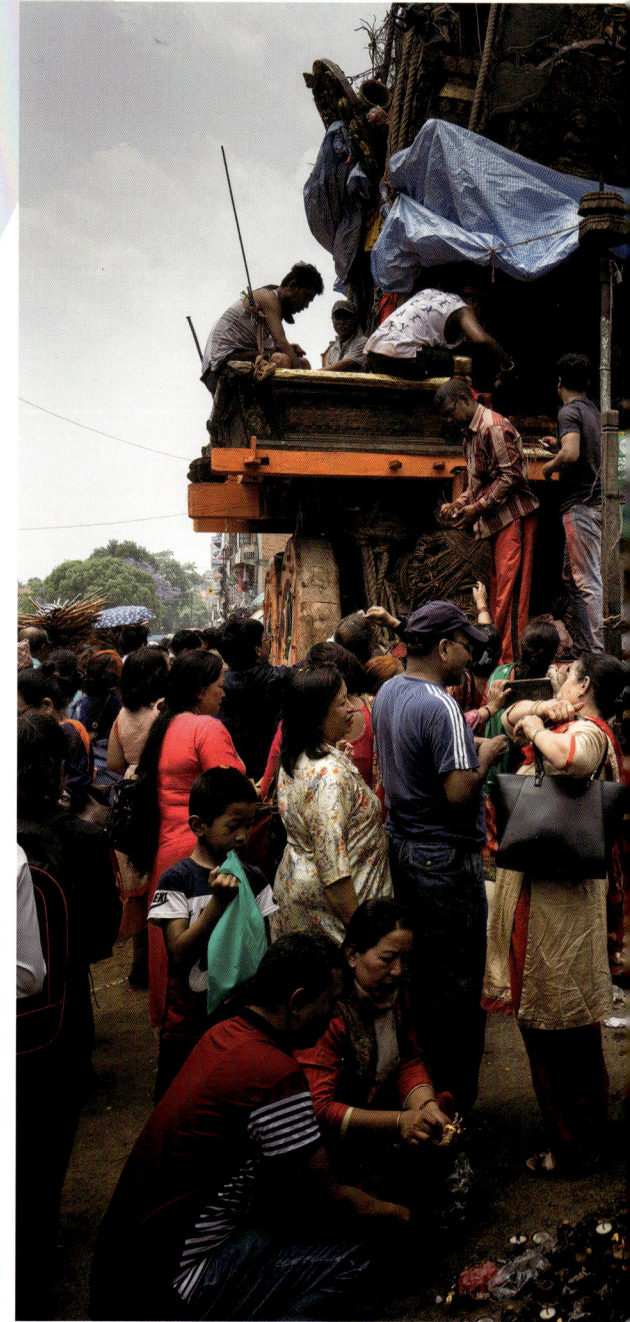

Kathmandu is the capital city of Nepal and is where every trip to Khumbu starts. It sits at 1400m in the bowl of Kathmandu Valley near the confluence of the Baghmati and Bishnumati rivers. It is surrounded by four major mountains: Shivapuri, Phulchoki, Nagarjun, and Chandragiri.

It is possibly the oldest continuously inhabited place in the world, founded in 723 by Raja Gunakamadeva. Its early name was Manju-Patan; the present name refers to a wooden temple (kath, "wood"; mandir, "temple") built from the wood of a single tree planted by Raja Lachmina Singh in 1596. A building that contains wood from the tree, still stands in the central square and is used for the accommodation of sādhus (Hindu holy men).

It is my favourite city – a chaotic, vibrant, colourful place, full of history and mystery. Go with the flow, don't rush, wander slowly around the hustle and bustle of UNESCO World Heritage Sites – Durbar Square, Swayambhunath, Boudhanath and Pashupatinath and the hundreds of narrow streets.

SĀDHUS / SĀDHVIS

Sādhus (male) and sādhvis (females) are highly respected in Hinduism and their life is solely dedicated to achieving moksha (liberation from the cycle of life, death, and rebirth) through meditation and contemplation of Brahman. Becoming a sādhu (male) or sādhvi (female) is the fourth and final phase in a Hindu's life – aśrama. The other three are studies, being a father and a pilgrim.

To become sādhu/sādhvis requires 'vairagya' where the person cuts all familial, societal and earthly attachments. It is a path followed by millions of people, but for most it is not a practical option. To become a holy person, first requires a guru. The student (sisya) must perform 'guruseva' (service) and the guru decides whether the person is eligible. There are many ways to be trained but all have the same goal – attaining moksha.

Sādhus generally wear simple clothing, such as saffron-coloured clothing, symbolising their renunciation of worldly possessions (sannyāsa). They are viewed as benefiting society and are supported by donations from many people , but they generally don't beg.

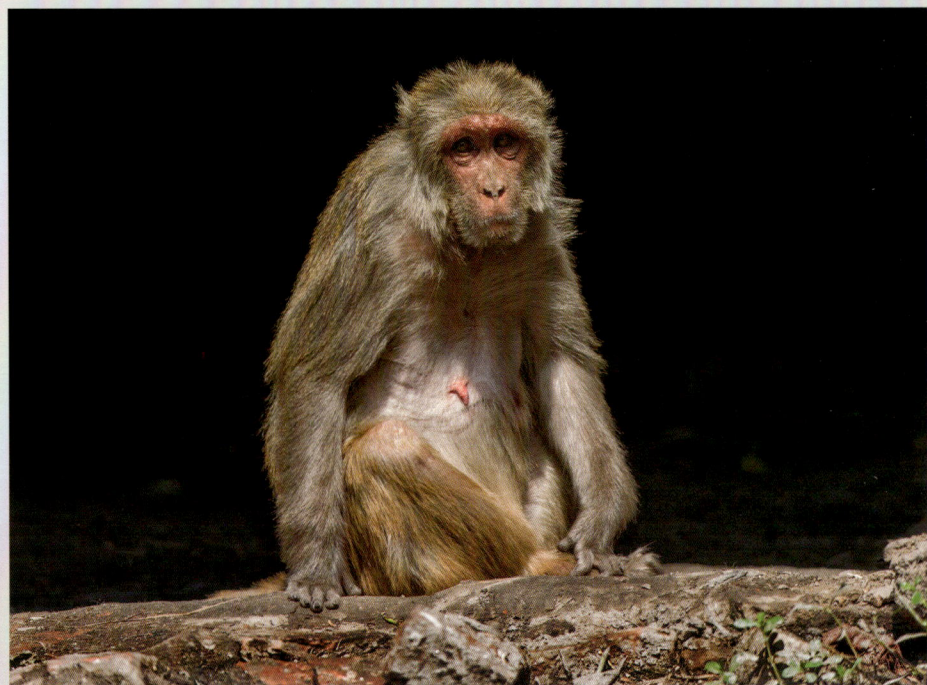

PHOTO LIST

PHOTOGRAPHY

EQUIPMENT

A Nikon Z6 and Z8 with a Z 24-120 f4, a Z 50mm and 85mm f1.8, a Nikon D850 with F20mm f1.8, 24-70mm f2.8, F80-200mm f4.

A Feisol Tripod with a Gitzo head.

Taking good photographs is understanding your subject and learning to see what is around you. It is about creating layers – an aesthetic layer, a subject layer, a moment layer and the the fourth layer which is the mystical alchemy that elevates a good photo to the great one.

Good light is fundamental to great images, but first of all you have to be there so get up early and go to bed late. Take your time pressing the shutter but don't delay when necessary. When you see something interesting ask yourself what is grabbing your attention in that scene or that person. Keep your camera handy, you will miss too many shots if it is in your rucksack. The large contrast range will always make exposures in the snowy mountains tricky. Expose to the right of the histogram, but take care not to clip the highlights.

If you would like to attend a workshop or photo trek then please get in contact ar@alunrichardson.co.uk

The hardest job in creating this book was selecting the images from thousands I had taken on many trips, to see more and buy prints go to:

www.alunrichardson.co.uk

GURKHAS

The British first encountered Gurkhas in 1814 during the Anglo-Nepalese War. The British admired their military abilities and honourable tactics, and began recruiting Gurkha troops in 1815. Gurkhas have been recruited into the British and Indian Army for over 200 years. They are renowned for their loyalty, professionalism and bravery, and have been awarded 13 Victoria Crosses. The Brigade of Gurkhas is the collective name for all the units in the British Army that are made up of Gurkha soldiers.

ABOUT THE GURKHA WELFARE TRUST (GWT)

In the late 1960s it was realised that a great number of Gurkha veterans and their dependants in Nepal were facing destitution in their old age. Many of the soldiers had served in World War Two; however they had not completed the 15 years' service required to qualify for a British Army Pension. After leaving the Army, thousands had returned to their home country to a life of hardship and poverty.

In 1970 an appeal was launched in 'The Times' newspaper, to support the veterans. The response by the British public was incredible and resulted in the creation of the GWT. Funds were distributed to Gurkha veterans widows through payment of a monthly "Welfare Pension" and the GWT continues to honour the legacy of these brave Gurkha soldiers by providing vital assistance to veterans, their families and communities in Nepal.

THE TRUST TODAY

The core focus of the GWT remains the relief of poverty and distress among Gurkha ex-servicemen and their dependants. We now have over 500 staff in Nepal operating from 21 Area Welfare Centres spread across traditional Gurkha recruiting areas and one in Darjeeling, India. These act as hubs from which our Pensioner Support Teams head out into the field to visit Gurkha veterans and widows in their own homes to provide financial aid and vital medical care. They may be travelling for days in 4x4 vehicles, on motorbikes or even on foot to reach pensioners in remote mountainous locations.

Over time the charity's remit has expanded to provide support to wider Gurkha and nepalese communities by providing access to clean water and education. Following the devastating earthquake of 2015 we have also made it a priority to ensure that our pensioners stay safe by building earthquake-resilient homes.

Since the launch of the first appeal we have been bowled over by the generosity and kindness of our supporters and thousands of veterans and their families now receive a pension and medical care, have a roof over their head, and live in communities with access to clean water and education. Dhanyabad – Thank you!

Top: We have been supporting veteran Chandraman Tamang with a pension and medical care since 1982. He proudly displays his medals including the Burma Star.
Right: Sergeant Dipprasad Pun

PHOTOGRAPHY

EQUIPMENT

A Nikon Z6 and Z8 with a Z 24-120 f4, a Z 50mm and 85mm f1.8, a Nikon D850 with F20mm f1.8, 24-70mm f2.8, F80-200mm f4.

A Feisol Tripod with a Gitzo head.

Taking good photographs is understanding your subject and learning to see what is around you. It is about creating layers – an aesthetic layer, a subject layer, a moment layer and the the fourth layer which is the mystical alchemy that elevates a good photo to the great one.

Good light is fundamental to great images, but first of all you have to be there so get up early and go to bed late. Take your time pressing the shutter but don't delay when necessary. When you see something interesting ask yourself what is grabbing your attention in that scene or that person. Keep your camera handy, you will miss too many shots if it is in your rucksack. The large contrast range will always make exposures in the snowy mountains tricky. Expose to the right of the histogram, but take care not to clip the highlights.

If you would like to attend a workshop or photo trek then please get in contact ar@alunrichardson.co.uk

The hardest job in creating this book was selecting the images from thousands I had taken on many trips, to see more and buy prints go to:

www.alunrichardson.co.uk

GURKHAS

The British first encountered Gurkhas in 1814 during the Anglo-Nepalese War. The British admired their military abilities and honourable tactics, and began recruiting Gurkha troops in 1815. Gurkhas have been recruited into the British and Indian Army for over 200 years. They are renowned for their loyalty, professionalism and bravery, and have been awarded 13 Victoria Crosses. The Brigade of Gurkhas is the collective name for all the units in the British Army that are made up of Gurkha soldiers.

ABOUT THE GURKHA WELFARE TRUST (GWT)

In the late 1960s it was realised that a great number of Gurkha veterans and their dependants in Nepal were facing destitution in their old age. Many of the soldiers had served in World War Two; however they had not completed the 15 years' service required to qualify for a British Army Pension. After leaving the Army, thousands had returned to their home country to a life of hardship and poverty.

In 1970 an appeal was launched in 'The Times' newspaper, to support the veterans. The response by the British public was incredible and resulted in the creation of the GWT. Funds were distributed to Gurkha veterans widows through payment of a monthly "Welfare Pension" and the GWT continues to honour the legacy of these brave Gurkha soldiers by providing vital assistance to veterans, their families and communities in Nepal.

THE TRUST TODAY

The core focus of the GWT remains the relief of poverty and distress among Gurkha ex-servicemen and their dependants. We now have over 500 staff in Nepal operating from 21 Area Welfare Centres spread across traditional Gurkha recruiting areas and one in Darjeeling, India. These act as hubs from which our Pensioner Support Teams head out into the field to visit Gurkha veterans and widows in their own homes to provide financial aid and vital medical care. They may be travelling for days in 4x4 vehicles, on motorbikes or even on foot to reach pensioners in remote mountainous locations.

Over time the charity's remit has expanded to provide support to wider Gurkha and nepalese communities by providing access to clean water and education. Following the devastating earthquake of 2015 we have also made it a priority to ensure that our pensioners stay safe by building earthquake-resilient homes.

Since the launch of the first appeal we have been bowled over by the generosity and kindness of our supporters and thousands of veterans and their families now receive a pension and medical care, have a roof over their head, and live in communities with access to clean water and education. Dhanyabad – Thank you!

Top: We have been supporting veteran Chandraman Tamang with a pension and medical care since 1982. He proudly displays his medals including the Burma Star.
Right: Sergeant Dipprasad Pun

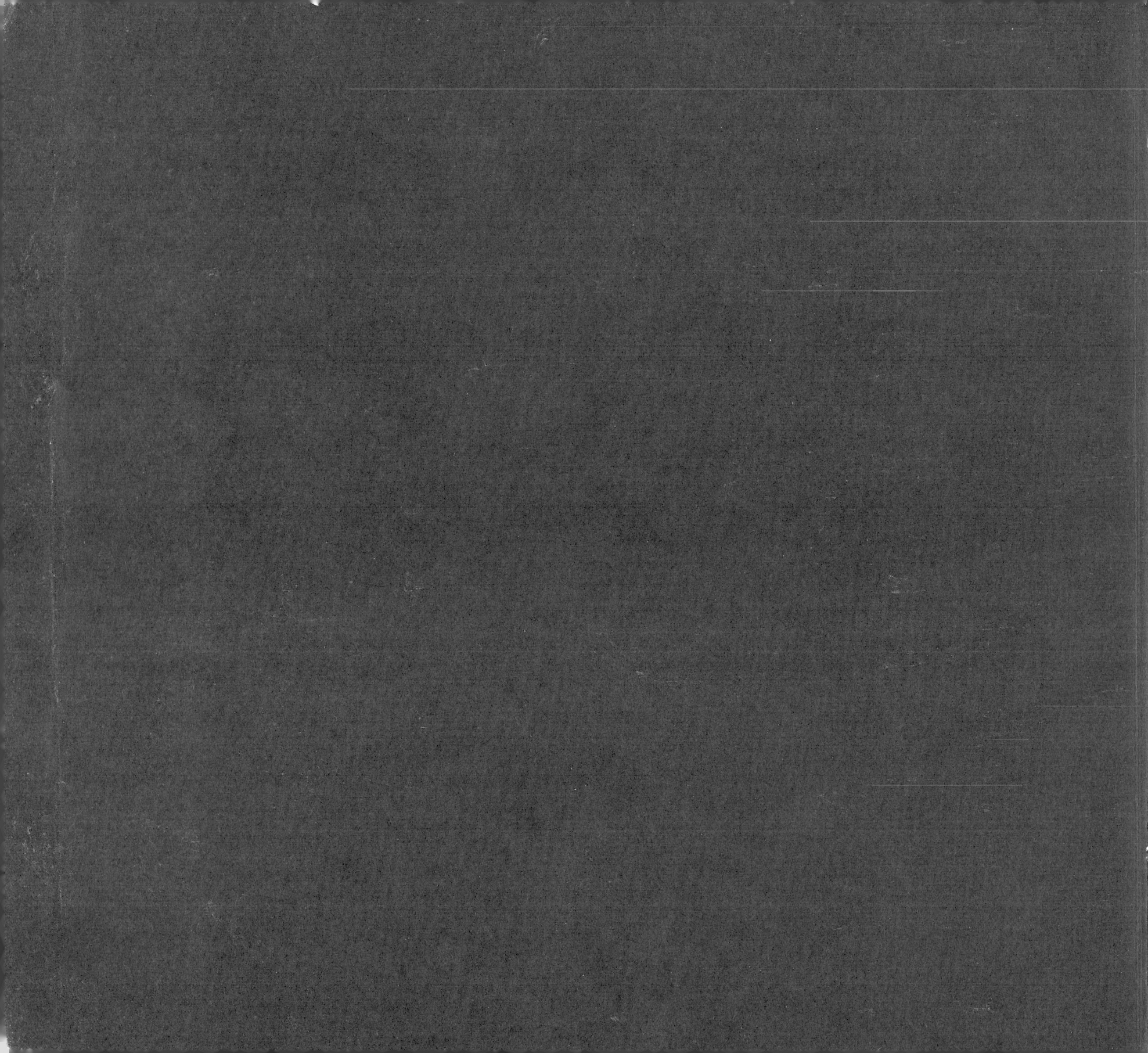